The Creative Use of Schizophrenia in Caribbean Writing

Dr. Viola Davis

caribbeanchapters

Second Edition. December, 2008
(First Edition published in 2001 by Intelek International)

Published by Caribbean Chapters
P.O. Box 4133, Speightstown, St. Peter, Barbados
Suite 246-122, 7805 NW 15th Street, Doral, Florida, 33126
www.caribbeanchapters.com

Send comments and/or questions
about this publication to
caribbeanchapters@gmail.com

Set in Garamond, Parchment and Jester

ISBN:
978-976-8219-63-3
paperback

Table of Contents

Foreword

This is not a critique. I am not so qualified to disturb all that rich, deep earth of words, of creative love and thought, passion and compassion found in Dr. Davis' effort. It would be an offence to use any of those so often polished mutterings that generally pass as supportive seeds, but are really smooth, shiny barren pebbles. In their dubious complexity, they neither flavour nor flower effort. I will not make a pretty, plastic 'scarecrow' out of any mis-understanding. I prefer to linger in this fertile place which Ms. Davis has ploughed in her artful sojourn entitled *The Creative Use of Schizophrenia in Caribbean Writing*.

This work is Dr. Davis' master's dissertation. It is an academic effort, but it does not 'kafuffle' the brain-box or 'cat-spraddle' reason. Rather, like any good piece of literature, it prompts that investigative process and encourages a fresh look at the conventions we entertain, especially about the literature of four of this region's post-independence visionaries: Edward Kamau Brathwaite of Barbados, Wilson Harris of Guyana, V.S. Naipaul of Trinidad and Tobago, and Derek Walcott of St. Lucia; and at West Indian literature in general. When I speak of West Indian literature, I include that popular voice nestled in the heartbeat of reggae and calypso music. At the sub-textual level, *The Creative Use of Schizophrenia in Caribbean Writing* provokes a connection with all of these voices.

Even though Dr. Davis does not entertain a popular style, we are connected through this new voice of the region's literati to a process which seeks to deepen our understanding of those three dualities that are present everywhere in Caribbean literature: self/other, freedom/servitude and exile/homecoming.

This outstanding work reminds us that 'the pleasure of exile' is a constant state of mind; a fateful journey of which George Lamming speaks, taking us to that same place where Bob Marley goes: *you running and you running but you can't hide from yourself*. What more forceful image of a split personality can there be than a man or woman running from his/her self? This image epitomises a disintegration of the emotional stability—a schizophrenia. It also creates a picture of a sick soul in the middle of a never-ending journey—Marley again: *one step forward two steps backwards*—always in the middle.

The Barbadian calypsonian Red Plastic Bag reminds us that the sickness of a 'middle-passage existence' is not an easily curable disease. When he 'sees his people suffer' it is not merely from an illness he supposes to be mental rather than physical, as in the case of a psychological enslavement which has received no better treatment than any other incurable illness like cancer or HIV/Aids, but 'Bag', like R.D. Laing, is taking us to a deeper place, to that place of a label that some people pin on other people under social circumstances. The cause to be found by the examination not of prospective diagnoses alone, but by the whole social context in which the psychiatric ceremonial (middle-class behaviour) is being conducted. And what is more middling than mulatto? Maybe schizophrenia is. And what is more schizophrenic than a people who are like half-baked, half-risen loaves, who are not done but spoilt, who are discarded by the master baker, indigestible to themselves?

Tony Thompson, Actor, Broadcaster

November, 2008

Preface

The inspiration for this thesis derives from Derek Walcott's reflection on his own work, and on the West Indian writer in general. He has written:

> '...and the only way to recreate this language was to share in the tortures of its articulation. This did not mean the jettisoning of 'culture' but, by the writer's making creative use of his schizophrenia, an electric fusion of the old and the new.'[1]

In an effort to understand Walcott's statement that schizophrenia could be an ingredient of the creative impulse, I have found that Walcott has imaginatively arrived at a concept of schizophrenia, albeit literary, which is corroborated by the psychiatrist R.D. Laing.

Laing believes that the schizophrenic must be seen in relation to his social context. He felt that the schizophrenic was reacting to the conflicts and stresses in his society, and had to adopt special strategies to live in what he perceived as an unlivable situation. The artist's response to the conflicts and stresses in his society is through his art. The Caribbean writer's expression of these conflicts and stresses is what I seek to examine in this thesis.

By referring to the works of E.K. Brathwaite, V.S. Naipaul, Wilson Harris and Derek Walcott, and examining what their works say to us, I have tried to trace a literature that is truly

1

Caribbean. In exploring the concept of 'making creative use of his schizophrenia' one gleans that almost everything had to be created out of the clash of cultures that finds expression in Caribbean writing, so that something uniquely Caribbean could emerge. Language, religion, politics, philosophy and above all, people, have become new creations. Yet the writer has to first unearth all the 'monsters' which lie beneath the ground of his being in order to create something whole and new.

'Monsters' such as racism, cultural imperialism, exploitation, philistinism, an inadequate view of history, the uncertain role of the Caribbean woman, all have been exposed. I have tried to focus on these hidden subterranean forces which sometimes precipitate the emotional disturbance which often is a characteristic of the schizophrenic, and which has gone into the making of Caribbean literature.

Brathwaite's concern with the African past is a plea for Afro-Caribbean man to affirm his 'African cargo'; to know and understand his past as a positive step to wholeness. Naipaul's quest for freedom exposes the conflicts of a Hindu Brahmin East Indian born in a predominantly black Trinidad, where a sense of deprivation, loss and alienation informs his work. Subtle shades of one form of racism (that between East Indians and Africans) emerge, attitudes spill over into relationships in the wider world of England and India.

Harris' contribution, the fulfilment of character in his novels, puts him squarely in the arena of the psychological-mythical writing. He convinces us that the artist's role is that of promoting the whole man, the authentic Caribbean man— the truly free person. Walcott's struggle to be at home in the world emerges as he exposes the peculiarly Caribbean conflict of the mulatto, whether of style or skin.

In this exploration of some Caribbean writers' works, what is revealed is the use they make of their 'schizophrenia'.

Introduction

There is now an accepted body of work which is designated as
'Caribbean Literature', in that it is literature of the Caribbean
placed squarely in geographical space, easily identifiable on
a map of the world. But Caribbean Literature is much more
complex than this geographical reality. It is also a product of
a peculiar historical, social, political and cultural mixture. The
Caribbean consists of 'People Who Came'[2] – this is now the
title of a West Indian History Series – people who came from
the old world willingly or unwillingly; people who came in the
name of conquest either exploiting or being exploited; people
of different ethnic origins, cultures and economic systems.

There were representatives of British, Dutch, French and
Spanish Imperialism, as well as African slave labour, East
Indian, Chinese and Portuguese indentured labour. These
were the 'reservoir of cheap labour, the material base
on which kingdoms of luxury of convenience would be
constructed elsewhere'.[3] It is this 'melting pot'[4] which Wilson
Harris sees as 'a strange and subtle goal'[5] and as a 'tradition of
the Americas.'[6] Wilson Harris' West Indies is more than just
islands, and for the purpose of the political concept of the
English-speaking Caribbean, includes the mainland territory
of Guyana:

> 'When I speak of the West Indies, I am thinking of
> overlapping contexts of Central and South America
> as well. For the mainstream of the West Indies in my

estimation possesses an enormous escarpment down which it falls, and I am thinking here of the European discovery of the New World and conquest of the ancient American civilizations which were themselves related by earlier and obscure levels of conquest.'[7]

This concept of the 'melting pot' makes at least one critic recall Harris' interest in 'alchemical symbolism', the search for a 'subtle evanescent reality',[8] the pursuit of which is a goal fraught with trauma, since (to pursue the metaphor) the 'metals' thrown into the pot were seen in terms of baser/ inferior; higher/superior races.

Fanon, in his analysis of the effects of conquest on the behaviour of the conquered, says:

'In the initial phase we have seen the occupying power legitimizing its domination by scientific arguments, the 'inferior race' being denied on the basis of race. Because no other solution is left it, the racialized social group tries to imitate the oppressor and thereby to deracialize itself. The inferior race denies itself as a different race. It shares with the 'superior race' the convictions, doctrines and other attitudes concerning it.

Having witnessed the liquidation of its system of reference, the collapse of its cultural patterns, the native can recognise with the occupant that 'God is not on his side'. The oppressor, through the inclusive and frightening characters of his authority, manages to impose on the native new ways of seeing and in particular a pejorative judgement with respect to his original forms of existing.'[8]

Two factors which emerge, which have frightening connotations for the individual native's psychic health are his 'denial of self' and the 'internalization of inferiority'. Add to this the black/white dichotomy and one can begin to talk in terms of pathology. Frantz Fanon has remarked that 'the negro is comparison.... he is constantly preoccupied with self-evaluation and with the ego-ideal.'[10]

Martin Carter, himself a West Indian writer, has noted, 'There are certain themes (in the West Indian novel) which are specifically Caribbean. I mean slavery and the quest for personal identity.'[11]

To quote Michael Gilkes, 'it was the Guyanese Mttelholzer who first raised the question of the role of heredity itself: the phenomenon of racial admixture and the cultural disorientation which lay beneath the West Indian's deep psychological need to define racial and cultural identity'.[12] There is the sense in which Caribbean Literature is unique. It seeks to come to terms with three main dualities:

 i. self/other
 ii. freedom/servitude
 iii. exile/homecoming

The quotations which follow suggest the extent to which these dualities have informed the imagination of our creative writers.

Derek Walcott writes:

'So that mongrel as I am, something prickles in me which I see the word Ashanti as with the word Warwickshire, both separately intimating my grandfathers' roots, both baptising this neither proud nor ashamed bastard, this hybrid, this West Indian.'[13]

And he describes his experience as:

'that wrestling contradiction of being white in mind and black in body, as if the flesh were coal from which the spirit like tormented smoke writhed to escape.'[14]

VS. Naipaul states that:

'Writers need a source of strength other than that which they find in their talent. Literary talent doesn't exist by itself, it feeds on a society and depends for its development on the nature of that society. What is true of my father is true of other writers of the region, we all in different ways discover that we stand nowhere. 'We being all islands in air': The words are from a poem in Derek Walcott's first locally published book. The writer begins with his talent, finds confidence in his talent but then discovers that it isn't enough that, in a society as deformed as ours, by the exercise of his talent he has set himself adrift...'[15]

What Naipaul is dealing with is the deprivation of talent – where there is no reciprocal reader. The writer therefore sets himself adrift from the society, because no one is clear about what he is doing. Harris, who is concerned with the Caribbean man's psyche pleads:

'Facism (and all that has come to imply in rigged elections etc.) is a disaster in the Third World as anywhere else, and makes all the more imperative the growth of a body of criticism, in dialogue with the nature of freedom.'[16]

And George Lamming adds:

> 'Ridicule and a habitual neglect were the social barriers which always threatened us with destruction. And in desperation we started on that fateful journey which had always been the saving doom of our people. We took flight. Hence, the phrase and paradox which would become a continuing source of argument, my own 'Pleasure of Exile.'[17]

Although my use of the term 'schizophrenia' is literary, Bleuler's discussion of the term is useful. In 1911 Bleuler coined the term schizophrenia. The word schizophrenia is derived from two Greek words and means a splitting of the personality.

The kind of splitting of the personality envisaged by the term schizophrenia is essentially one of feeling, a disintegration of the emotional stability of the patient, and it is impossible to imagine any single term which could better indicate and exemplify the process of the disease.

Schizophrenia can best be regarded as a form of mental illness displayed by human beings subject to various kinds of stress and meeting it with various constitutional handicaps which even now are not fully understood.[18] Walcott's 'wrestling contradiction' is the stress from which comes the recognition of a certain pathology.

> 'In that simple schizophrenic boyhood one could lead two lives, the interior life of poetry, the outward life of

action and dialect.'[19]

Walcott's two lives may also reflect the stratification which takes place within the society. The life within the lower middle-class household and the life of the street. There was a gap between the two, the lower, middle-class home where poetry, painting, reading are encouraged and have positive social value, and the life of the poor, the life of action and dialect. This is the life which informs his work as a writer. The split is reflected in the social order.

The various kinds of stress Caribbean writers would have to meet, and how they have met them, is the subject of this thesis. Derek Walcott's phrase 'making creative use of his schizophrenia' gives the impetus for an exploration of schizophrenia as an ingredient in creativity.

R.D. Laing, in discussing schizophrenia, states:

'In using the term schizophrenia, I am not referring to any condition that I suppose to be mental rather than physical, or to an illness, like pneumonia, but to a label that some people pin on other people under social circumstances. The 'cause' of schizophrenia is to be found by the examination not of prospective diagnoses alone, but of the whole social context in which the psychiatric ceremonial is being conducted.'[20]

What Laing and other modem psychiatrists are dealing with here is that the 'schizophrenic' must be seen in relation to his social context. I believe that this is also Derek Walcott's perception. His work, like the work of other Caribbean writers, springs from a particular social context which generated the conflict and the stress which have precipitated the creative impulse.

Caribbean writing might be viewed as the way in which writers dealt with their experience of the Caribbean world. The writers themselves were compromisers in the society; they quite often shared the assumptions of the society. Thus some Caribbean writers have been ambivalent about their status. On the one hand, their experience of themselves as educated, cultured and sensitive West Indians, contradicted the assumptions of the society they themselves shared—a society of people of inferior status as colonials and descendants of African slave or indentured labour. They were therefore forced either to reject an untenable position or to accept the societal assumptions and adjust to this distressing definition of self.

To accommodate oneself to a society that is to one's experience dysfunctional is in itself alienating, even dangerous. Thus the refusal, by silence, of the majority of our people in the Caribbean to face up to the fact that the society is dysfunctional, means that they have compromised their authenticity in a way that the creative artist cannot and will not. This is the sense in which the artist throws light on what is hidden from the less discerning.

In this context, his insights can be labeled 'schizophrenic'. 'They will see that what we call 'schizophrenia' was one of the forms in which, often through ordinary people, the light began to break through the cracks in our all-too-closed minds.[21]

Wilson Harris' concern with vision and his use of words such as 'light,' 'enlightenment', 'seeing eye', 'blind-eye' are in this context a quest for the authentic man; a desire to open our

10

minds to other possibilities of being in the world. There is also the lesson one can learn from the schizoid personality that bears special reference to my thesis: that is that one's sense of 'being at home in the world' is a painful process for those whose sense of the world makes them peculiarly isolated and alone. The artist's vision may prevent him from always being at ease in his society.

'The term schizoid refers to an individual the totality of whose experience is split in two ways; in the first place there is a rent in his relation with his world; and in the second there is a disruption of his relation with himself. Such a person is not able to experience himself 'together with' others or 'at home in' the world, but on the contrary he experiences himself in despairing aloneness and isolation. Moreover, he does not experience himself as a complete person but rather as 'split' in various ways, perhaps as a mind more or less tenuously linked to a body, as the two or more selves and so on.'[22]

Walcott, in his visionary way, expresses in his poem 'Homecoming' all the despairing aloneness and isolation of the writer who discovers that being at home in the world is a painful process, and that wholeness and healing can only come through wrestling with the contradictions, in a fight to harmonise the different selves. Thus Walcott's interior life is the life of reflection and disillusionment, while the outward life of action and dialect is the life of the folk.

'...that image is the old colonial grimace of the laughing nigger steelbandsman, carnival masker, calypsonian and limbo dancer.'[23] It is the folk who inform his work as a writer.

'Years ago, watching them, and suffering as you watched, you professed silently the clarity of a language which they could not speak, until you, suffering like the language, felt superior, estranged.'[24]

This leading of two lives is also neatly documented by Garth St. Omer.

'I know now that it is only we, the serious uncertain masqueraders, fearful of the laughter of those who observe us who commit excesses. Eager to convince, we intensify our posturing until the impersonation we intended as reality for others begins to assume reality for us. We play less and less for those who watch us and in the end, it is ourselves only that we fool. It is then, that more than ever we need to continue to perform, otherwise our world ends.'[25]

Of course Paul's personality, the voice of 'J. Black Bam and the Masqueraders' finally disintegrates:

'Months later when I decided to become mad, it was to preserve my identity whole for myself that I reflected its bits for others to look upon.'[26]

Paradoxical as it may sound, Paul's decision 'to become mad' is a positive step towards psychic health and well-being. Again, V.S. Naipaul, in his foreword to a collection of short stories by his father Seepersad Naipaul, *The Adventures of Guradeva and Other Stories*, states:

'One day in 1934, when he was twenty-eight, five years after he had been writing for the Guardian, some months after Gault McGowan had left the paper and Trinidad, my father looked in the mirror and thought he couldn't see himself. It was the beginning of a long mental illness that caused him for a time to be unemployed, and as dependent as he had been in his childhood. It was after his recovery that he began writing stories and set himself the goal of the book.'[27]

The phrase 'couldn't see himself' is a startling metaphor of the condition of so many Caribbean people, and one which clarifies not only the condition of Schizophrenia, but very importantly, the sort of creativity that can come out of the psychological stresses which the individual must face. Finally, it is worth noting that Derek Walcott dedicated his poem 'Homecoming: Anse La Raye' to Garth St. Omer. In it he shares St. Omer's sense of the futility of the exile who returns and finds that nothing seems to have changed:

'There are no rites for those who have returned.'[28]

Walcott makes the discovery that one is 'no longer at ease', that home has not so much to do with 'place', a physical spot. Like Harris, he discovers:

'the education of freedom....
the need to lose the base concretion men seek to impose
when they talk of one's 'native'
and (or another's as if it were fixed and anchored in place.'[29]

And he comments:

'Today, I am your poet, yours, all this you
then knew, but never guessed you'd come

to know there are homecomings without home.'[30]

This thesis proposes to examine and to explore in depth this rich vein, the creative use of schizophrenia in Caribbean Literature. Walcott says it like this:

> 'And the only way to recreate this language was to share in the torture of its articulation. This did not mean jettisoning of 'culture' but by the writer's making creative use of his schizophrenia, an electric fusion of the old and the new.'[31]

Since one cannot divorce Caribbean Literature from its historical, racial or economic moorings, concerns which arise out of this literature must in a fundamental way question the whole concept of history, of ethnicity, exploitation and culture. One may find that there are levels of servitude or alienation which must be confronted. One must examine why certain limitations of place, limitations of vision, limitations to the full functioning or integrated personalities bedevil us. One must re-examine the ambivalences of attitudes toward one's past and one's ethnic origins.

Slavery and indenture are integral to our history. Who were the free people, who are the free people now? By what measure must we measure their freedom? No one could be truly free in an oppressive society – no one can be truly free where the majority of the population are ruthlessly exploited, whether this exploitation is on grounds of race, rationalized on some archaic notion of racial superiority, or whether this exploitation is simply exploitation of labour. Cultural or ethnic imperialism is as binding and limiting to the one who imposes it as to the one on whom it is imposed. In order to keep anyone in blinkers in terms of that person's self image, one has to live in fear that the blinkers could be or may be removed.

Caribbean writers are as much victims of their world as the people they write about. In order to be the fully integrated creative individuals that we all must be in the process of becoming, these attitudes and concepts must be brought to light, must be exposed, dug out and be allowed to bear the light not only of scrutiny, but the light of understanding and vision. This study seeks to highlight some of the sources of the West Indian artist's schizophrenia. In isolating the symptoms it hopes to pinpoint the "constitutional handicaps, with which the 'patient' is meeting his 'stress situations'." It may lead to the unearthing or repossession of the buried self, the 'denied self.' It may mean that one does not allow oneself to be defined by others. It may lead to the search for an authentic self. The choice is either as Walcott sees the West Indian's mind:

'Preferring to take its revenge in nostalgia to narrow its eyelids in schizophrenic daydream of an Eden that existed before its exile.'[32]

Or as Harris sees it:

'A major task of creativity is to penetrate complex self-deceptions as well as the complex values with which we have invested objects or orders that we have come to take for granted.'[33]

One

Creative Use of Schizophrenia:
The Interior Life of Poetry;
The Outward Life of Action and Dialect

'And the only way to recreate this language was to share in the torture of articulation. This did not mean the jettisoning of culture but by the writer's making creative use of his schizophrenia, an electric fusion of the old and the new.'[34]

Derek Walcott

'The artist is a human being who uses usually one, sometimes more than one medium of communication with exceptional force and skill.'[35]

C.L.R. James

'Language is not a mere tool, one of the many which man possesses, on the contrary it is only language that affords the very possibility of standing in the openness of the existent.'[36]

Heidegger

The West Indian writer is placed in a very interesting relationship to the language which he uses. Walcott puts it very succinctly:

> 'I have entered the house of literature as a houseboy
> filched as the slum child stole
> as the young slave appropriated these heirlooms
> temptingly left with the Victorian homilies of Noli
> Tangere'[37]

The fact that West Indian writers came to Literature in a formal sense through Western European classical writing is acknowledged here by Walcott. Yet the language of the literature is informed by a speech which is oral, and is influenced by the King James version of the Bible. The language appropriated willingly or unwillingly bears the stamp of a pastiche of accretions. From the patois of the once French dominated islands to the African, Indian, Portuguese, Spanish components, all contribute to the pot pourri which has become a West Indian form of expression. Whether it is English based, French based, Spanish based or Dutch based, it is most certainly a distinct form of expression, distinctly New World.

Gerald Moore recognises this West Indian contribution to the English Language thus:

> 'Thus, whether his ancestors be from Africa, India, Europe or China or any mixture of these, he has to learn the shape and feeling of his new Caribbean environment and make himself a part of it. He also, unless his is a fairly new arrival, has English as his mother tongue, albeit an English stamped by the islands, with many structures, sequences and words derived from non-English sources. For the vast majority of West Indians today, of whatever

colour, English is their sole language, and it is through English alone that they can hope to define themselves and their society'.[38] He recognises that something has been created here.

Brathwaite expresses the problem thus:

'My tongue is heavy with new language, but I cannot give birth speech.'[39]

'The process of recreating a language is not an easy one.
I
must be given words to shape my name
to the syllables of trees
I
must be given words to refashion futures
like a healer's hand
I
must be given words so that the bees
in my blood's buzzing brain of memory
will make flowers, will make flocks of birds
will make sky, will make heaven,
the heaven open to the under stone and
the volcano and the unfolding land
It is not, it is not
it is not enough, to be silent
to be semicolon, to be semicolony.

Fling me the stone
that will confound the void
find the rage
and I will raze the colony
fill me with words
and I will blind your God.

18

Att
Att
Attibon

Attibon Legba, Attibon Lega,
Ouvri bayi pou'moi
Ouvri bayi pou'moi'[40]

For Brathwaite, recreating the language is essential, if he is to express his peculiar experience as an Afro-West Indian, if he is to determine his own future, heal the psychic wounds and function creatively. Yet there is a language of action which gives birth to a language of images and words. 'Razing the Colony' is a political, not a literary matter; and it is perhaps, almost certainly this failure to transform our world by action which has aborted the birth of an authentic language of feeling. In this connection, it can and should be argued that the writers are still casualties of a certain political and social formation. Their art becomes a form of therapy and their critics function as the detectives of symbols.

Walcott talks of 'a language that went beyond mimicry; a dialect which had the force of revelation as it invented names for things; one which finally settled on its own mode of inflection; and which began to create an oral culture of chants, jokes, folk songs and fables.'[41]

Of course, Walcott could have added calypsos. Note how he used the tone and rhythm of the Trinidadian language with the added touch of calypso insouciance in Joker of Seville.

Ace of Death:

Now whether Juan gone down to Hell
Or up in Heaven, I cannot tell
Whether he gone down to Hell
Or up to heaven, death will not tell
But the truest joke he could play
Is to come back to us one day
Because if there's resurrection,
Death is the joker.
Sans humanité[42]

Michael Fabre, in an article on Walcott, notes:

'After rendering in prose (dramatic or otherwise) in
Dream on Monkey Mountain, the very tone of his people's
experience, he has succeeded in 'Another Life' in creating
a poetic language which is tonally one with that of his
own people, which is deeply attuned to his personal
growth and yet immediately universal.'[43]

What is relevant in this observation is "the very tone of his
people's experience", for surely the writer in the Caribbean is
simply returning the society to itself.

Walcott is committed to his muse: "We were blest with a
virginal unpainted world with Adam's task of giving things
their names."[44] By struggling to name things, and to be a
compassionate witness to a community, it was important that
we participate in the 'enduring sound' they shared together.

'I watch the vowels curl from the tongue of the
carpenter's plane
Resinous, fragrant

Labials of our forests,
Over the plain wood
The back crouched,
The vine - muscled wrist,
Like a man rowing,
Sweat - fleck on blond cedar
The smell of our own speech,
The smell of baking bread
Of drizzled asphalt, this odorous cedar.
After the rain the rinsed shingles shone
Resinous as the smell of country sweat,
Of salt crusted fisherman.
Christ, to shake off the cerecloths,
To stride from the magnetic sphere of legends
From the gigantic myth.'[45]

In an interview with John Thieme for Caribbean Contact, March 1980, Harris says:

'In savage cultures the beginning does not lie in the word, as in St. John's gospel. The beginning lies in the image in the gestures, in the hieroglyphic painting in the sculpture, in the mask and, when one comes to metaphor, one has the sense that language may have its roots in the way images broke their moorings to come into one physical consciousness and metaphor is at the heart of this mutation, because this mutation would seem to be an infinite descent into the world. When one says for example, the sun is a rose, one is involved, I would suggest in an unnameable center of light that exists between the sun and the rose.

The peculiarity of this is that it seems to me to suggest that one lives in a world where change is real. There's a tendency in us to think that the ground of reality is changeless. The ground of reality in an absolutely ultimate sense may be changeless, but it remains for us something which is unnameable, something which cannot be structured and therefore as we move into it, we are drawn to sense a capacity for change, real change.'[46]

He continues in the interview to explain the connection between painting and language. He refers to Da Silva Da Silva of Da Silva Da Silva's Cultivated Wilderness:

'So the paintings that Da Silva enters into are ways of suggesting that the language we use is never perfectly transparent, but the language nevertheless, can carry within it layers of illumination that mutate and come to the surface and that means that a work of imagination has a strange life which goes far deeper than the historical framework or decade in which it is set.'[47]

Harris realizes the difficulty of using language to clarify experience. Sometimes language obscures rather than enlightens, yet the creative writer, particularly the West Indian writer, has a responsibility to use language to promote genuine change in the human person.

Harris sees the West Indian artist in these terms: The West Indian artist therefore has a central theme or symbol and that symbol is man, the human person, as opposed to the European artist whose symbol is masses and materials."

'And when the artist looks at this human person he must deal with his 'obsessions' his 'conflicts' but also with 'the rhythms within the welter of his existence. He also has to articulate for the inarticulate in the way he sees most fit.'[48]

'Language for him therefore was 'a vision of consciousness, as if what one dreams of in the past is there with a new reality so expressive before, because nothing stands now to block the essential intercourse of its parts; however irrelevant'. We have this concept of Harris' use of language as a vision of consciousness', a free floating exercise in tapping the unconscious. This, of course, is responsible for the curious juxtapositions of words, and the dream-like quality of much of Harris' language, since images proliferate and metaphor seems to be more spontaneous than the word.'[49]

Harris also justifies the curious juxtaposition of words in order to bring into sharp focus the disturbance created by opposed conditions, and some of his 'opposed conditions' are the very essence of his concerns. These concerns are freedom and servitude; oppression and unfulfilment.

There is also the problem of dialect and Standard English. Dialect represents on the one hand the language of 'the folk' and Standard English the language of 'the privileged.' Thus the writer has to rediscover and reinforce the language of consciousness:

'We live in a twilight situation which half remembers, half forgets. As such the language of consciousness has to literally rediscover and reinforce itself in the face of accretions of accent and privilege the burden of 'sacred' usage or onesidedness.'[50]

It is the duty of the writer to innovate, to throw fresh and refreshing light on past and present experiences.

What will remain for many years to come as a unique concept of language is Harris' theory of language as transforming inner and outer formal categories of experience, earlier and representative modes of speech itself, the still life resident in painting and sculpture as such, even music which one ceases to hear. The peculiar reality of language provides a medium to see in consciousness the 'free' motion, and to 'hear with' consciousness the 'silent' flood of sound by a continuous inward revisionary and momentous logic of potent explosive images evoked in the mind.[51]

Harris may have experienced language in these terms because he is a native of a vast country with whose interior he was familiar. This confrontation with nature in its immensity and unfathomableness compared with the 'cosmic frailty of man' must have had a profound effect on his perception of reality. The continental vision has its own rewards; so does the islander's vision; yet they both speak of specific terrors; either the terrors of man's frailty or of man's barbarity.

This exploration of the creative approach to language highlights the challenge which language presents to the writers. Language is the tool which with great difficulty must be fashioned to illumine, to shed light on the hitherto unexplored recesses of Caribbean Man's psyche. It must in so doing 'refashion futures' yet it must be tonally one with the people's experience.

Two

Brathwaite and the African Presence in the Caribbean

If one looks at schizophrenia in the context of a 'split personality', Brathwaite undoubtedly underscores the conflict of the 'divided self' of the Afro-West Indian. He reflects the impossible situation in which Afro-West Indians found themselves in the colonial era. There was the total denial of their Africanness in the culture from which they sprung, thus the Afro-West Indian was psychologically two people: the slave without a past, and the African with some racial memories which manifested themselves in various ways.

Brathwaithe seeks wholeness by establishing an African basis of personality from which one can grow.

Brathwaite writes about the West Indian's rootlessness thus:

'It is a spiritual inheritance from slavery and the long story before that of the migrant African moving from the lower Nile across the desert to the Western ocean only to meet the Portuguese and a history that was to mean the middle passage, America and a rootless sojourn in the Caribbean sea.

> This dichotomy expresses itself in the West Indian through
> a certain psychic tension, an excitability, a definite feeling
> of having no past, of not really belonging (which some
> prefer to call adaptability) and finds relief in laughter (and
> more seriously) in movement, dance, cricket, carnival,
> emigration.'[52]

Brathwaite's West Indians are essentially Blacks of African
descent. I suppose this is understandable since Brathwaite is a
Barbadian, and Barbados' population is probably the nearest
to a homogeneous society in the Caribbean. Traditionally, the
majority have been the descendants of African slaves and the
rest of European descendants, mainly British; of course this is
a far cry from Harris' Guiana which is a heterogenous society,
and one is drawn to a much deeper 'ground of experience'.

Brathwaite's *The Arrivants,* a New World Trilogy, consists of
Rights of Passage, *Masks*, and *Islands*. In these three books he
explores the experiences and psychology of people who are
neophytes in the new world. They have had to earn their
status in the new world. They have had to die to the Old
World of Africa to be reborn to the New World of America
and the Caribbean. The initiation into the new world has been
fraught with all the paradox and ambiguity of their condition
as neophytes, and Rights of Passage looks at rites which
accompany these changes:

> 'Van Gennep has shown that all rites of transition are
> marked by three phases; separation, margin (or linen),
> and aggregation. The first phrase of separation comprises
> symbolic behaviour, signifying the attachment of the

individual or group; either from an earlier fixed point in the social structure or a set of cultural conditions ('a state') during the intervening liminal period the state of the ritual subject (the 'passenger') is ambiguous; he passes through a realm that has few or none of the attributes of the past or coming state, in the third phase the passage is consumated.'[53]

Thus in *Rights of Passage*, we trace the phases, separation from Africa through marginal status in the New World via all those migrations and journeys to acceptance that, 'There is no turning back.' 'The passage is consummated.' We are here for whatever it is worth as a people,

> '...for our blood mixed
> soon with their passion in sport
> in indifference, in anger
> will create new soils, new souls new ancestors.'[54]

A further structurally negative characteristic of transitional beings is that they have nothing. They have no status, property, insignia, secular clothing, rank, kinship, position, nothing to demarcate them structurally from their fellows.[55]

> '...the paths we shall never remember
> again, Atumpan talking and the largest branches,
> all the tribes of Ashanti dreaming the dream
> of Tutu, Anokye and the Golden Stool, built
> in Heaven for our nation by the work
> of lightning and the brilliant adze; and now nothing
> nothing.[56]

And yet there is hope that there will be a cultural fusion. Though Tom's survival depends on his apparent subservience, he hopes that his children's vision will encompass and include all the components of a heterogeneous heritage that the conquerors and the conquered cultures would become integrated.

> '...hoping my children's eyes
> will learn
> not green alone
> not Africa alone
> not dark alone
> not fear alone
> but Cortez, and Drake
> Magellan, and that Ferdinand
> the sailor, who pierced the salt seas to this land.'[57]

The anguish and agony of deracinated West Indians journeying from one continent to another are captured in the poem 'The Journeys'. The broken words, stops, starts, the one word, one letter lines are visual representations of the broken dreams, the disillusionment after arrivals and departures, the broken promises. The poem reads like a geography lesson. The journey of the Middle Passage is repeated in reverse this time from New World to the Old World of Europe.

> The Journey:

> 'E-
> gypt
> in A-frica
> Mesopo
> tamia
> Mero-
> e.
> the Nile

silica
glass
and britle
Sa-
hara, Tim-
buctu, Gao
the hills of
Ahafo, winds
of the Ni-
ger, Kumasi
and River
down the
coiled Congo
and down
that black river
that tides us to hell
Hell
in the water
brown
boys of Bushongo
drowned in the
blue and the bitter
salt of the wave-gullied
Ferdinand's sea
Soft winds
to San Salvador, Christo-
pher, Christ and no Noah
or dove to promise us grim
though it was, the simple sal-
vation of love. And so it was Little
Rock, Dall-
as, New Orleans, Santiago
De Cuba, the miles
of unfortunate islands; the
Saints and the Virgins, L'Ouvertures Haiti

ruined by greed and the slow
growing green of its freedom; golden Guiana:
Potaro
leaping in light liquid amber
in Makonaima's perpetual falls. And as if
the exhaustion of this wasn't all – Egypt,
Meroe, the Congo and all –
in the fall we reached Detroit, Chicago and Den-
ver; and then it was New
York, selling news-
papers in Brooklyn and Harlem,
Then Capetown and Rio; remember how we
took Paris by storm; Sartre, Camus, Picasso and
all?
But where are the dreams
of that bug happy, trash-
holstered tropical bed
when Uncle Tom lived
and we cursed him? This
the new deal for we black
grinning jacks? Lights
big like bubbies but we
still in shaks?'[58]

Brathwaite salutes the everlasting spirit of survival in man.
The resilience of the blues is there. However bad the situation
becomes one 'keeps on keeping on.' The ananse-type figure is
there 'coursing his own manoeuvres.[59]

'So went the black
hatted Zoot-
suited watch-
chained dream

of the Panama boys
and the hoods
from Chicago.'[60]

But there are also those who reject 'Babylon.' They reject
European cultural imperialism and turn towards an Africa
they have romantically created. Brathwaite captures the
rhythm of Jamaican dialect and particularly the Rastafarians'
Biblical style of speech—the inversions—

'...an' who fears most I...'

Interestingly enough, Babylon is not the only thing to fear,
but the 'clean face browns' are also fearsome. Here is the
historical deep-seated antagonism between mulattos and
blacks in the New World.

'And I
Rastafar-I
in Babylon's boom
town, crazed by the moon
and the peace of this chalice, I
prophet and singer, scourge
of the gutter, guardian
Trench Town, the Dungle and Young's
Town, rise and walk through the now silent
streets of affliction, hawks eyes
hard with fear, with
affection, and hear my people
cry, my people
shout
Down down
white
man con

man, brown
man, down
down full
man, frown-
ing fat
man. That
white black
man. That
lives in
the town.
An' who fears most I.'[61]

But by and large, there is the recognition that the West Indian
has gone through his *rites de passage* and is now a recognised
member of the new world. He is also free to create his own
'monsters.'

'Now slave no more
now harbour-
less no more. He forges
from his progress
flame. New iron masters:
brilliant concrete crosses -
look he bears - to crucify this freedom'[62]

In *Masks* there is a return to 'ruins' and 'relics'.

'Epic structure is employed only in 'Masks' which bears
some affinity in theme, tone and surprisingly enough in
rhythm, to Anglo Saxon poetry. In 'Masks', the wandering
consciousness of the excited African picks its painful
way through the ruins and relics and lost cities of an
identifiable but disastrous past.'[63]

Prelude

Out
of this
bright
sun, this
white plague
of heaven
this leaven-
ing heat
of the seven
kingdoms.
Songhai, Mali,
Chad, Ghana
Tim-
buctu, Volta
and the bitter
waste
that was
Ben-
in, comes
this shout
comes
this song.
Gong-Gongs
throw pebbles in the rout-
ed pools of silence; news
ripples reach the awakened Zu-
lus: Chaka tastes
the sale blood of the bitter
Congo and all Africa
is one, is whole; nim-
tree shaded in Ghana,
in Chad, Mali
the shores of the cooling kingdoms.'[64]

There is African history, all this is new to West Indians who were either brought up on British history or knew of African history from the European's point of view. We go back to proud, stable societies, whose life and ritual are disturbed by conquest by Arabs, by Portuguese and the Christians' God.

'Axum
With the help of the Caliph
of Heaven, who in heaven
and earth conquers all;
I, El Hassan, son of Amida,
King of Axum
of Halem, Hemer, Rayden and
Salhem;
made war on the Boba;
fought at Takazi, by the ford
of Kernalke; burnt town, destroyed
villages, pillaging
houses and temples
whether of stone or of straw
did not matter; splattered

blood in the corn;
burnt their altars of horn,
bronx and cooper; threw
their dark wooden gods in the river
and the next day rowed on
till we reached the Red River....'[65]

The plunder of Africa can partly be accounted for by the naivety and trust of the people:

'And beware
cried Akyere

do not trust strangers.'[66]

How often did this warning go unheeded to the chagrin, mortification and shame of a people? The gods have failed the people, there is fear and confusion.

'Why did the god's
stool you gave us from pride
foreign tribes' bibles
the Christian god's hunger.'[67]

And one hopes that a people would learn from a disastrous experience.

'I am learning
let me succeed
I am learning
let me succeed.'[68]

And we come to *Islands*. A quotation from James Baldwin's *Tell Me How Long the Train's Been Gone*. Sets the mood for *Islands*. 'The Children of Sisyphus'[69], immediately comes to mind:

'It was as though after indescribable, nearly mortal effort, after grim years of fasting and prayer, after the loss of all he had and after having been promised by the Almighty that he had paid the price and no more would be demanded of his soul, which was harboured now; it was as though in the midst of his joyful feasting and dancing, crowned and robed, a messenger arrived to tell him that a great error had been made, and that it was all to be done again.'[70]

The first poem in *Islands*, 'Jah' suggests 'linkages', 'bridges', and many musical images: 'trumpets', 'saxophones stop', 'drummer nerves', 'bluenote', 'crackednote', 'Panama worksong', 'guitar springs', suggesting musical links with the African past. Alongside these images are also those suggesting flight, but also decadence and discord 'eagles crook neck', 'vulture talons', 'hummingbird trees',

> '...and we float, high up over the sighs of the city, like a fish in a gold water world....'

But so much is lost,

> '...There are no chiefs in the village.'

The gods have been forgotten or hidden, buried with a sense of shame and guilt.

> 'A prayer poured on the ground with water,
> with rum, will not bid them come
> back. Creation has burned to a spider
> It peeps over the hills with the sunrise.
> But prefers to spin webs in the trees.
> The sea is a divider. It is not a life giver
> Time's river.'[71]

The poet laments the scourge of insularity, the sense of separation, the loss of direction of the inhabitants of the islands. There are no chiefs in the village the gods; have been forgotten or hidden. The sense of community is lost, there is no moral consensus, individualism is rampant.

Yet the indigenous religions of the Caribbean remind us of what we might have lost. 'Shepherd' is a poem which speaks of 'possession,' the anguish of creation. One has to be possessed, find oneself in a new relation with earth, the source of one's being for the dumb to speak.

Pocamania, Shango, Tie Head religions, these break the barriers erected between man's feeling nature and his reason, the body/soul dichotomy, It is a genuine breakthrough to creativity.

'The dumb speaks...'

Just as something new is created in these religions, so carnival, steelband, are new cultural forms:

'Jou'vert
Making
with their
rhythms some-
thing torn
and new.'[72]

Out of the crucible of suffering is created the limbo dance. Out of the bitterness of the Middle Passage experience, an attestation to the resilience of the survivors. The poem 'Caliban,' parts of which can be sung, since Brathwaite uses the rhythm and music of what has become a night club act— limbo.

'limbo
limbo like me
long dark deck and the water surrounding me
long dark deck and the silence is over me
limbo

limbo like me
stick is the whip
and the dark deck is slavery
limbo
limbo like me
drum stick knock and the darkness is over me
knees spread wide
and the water is hiding me
limbo
limbo like me
knees spread wide
and the dark ground is under me.'

Brathwaite's 'Rites' is a very humourous dialect poem. It is strange mixture, it recounts one of the 'rites' of the society—cricket; a British middle-class game played and enjoyed by mainly dialect-speaking working class West Indians, transforming the game altogether, into something sparkling and exciting. British cricket played with West Indian dialect exuberance.

Rites

'Clyde back pun he back foot
an' prax!
Is through extra cover an' four red runs all de way
'You see dat shot?' the people was showin'
'Jesus Christ, man, wunna see dat shot?'
All over de groun' fellers shakin' hands wid each
other
as if they wheelin' de willow
as if was them had the power
one man run out pun de field wid a red fowl cock
goin' quawk, quawk, quawk in 'e han?

Would 'a give it to Clyde right then an' right there
If a police hadn't stop 'e.'

Note the onomatopaeic words, the excitement of creating a
language 'prax' 'quawk.'

'But I say it once, an', I say it again
when things goin' good you cahn touch
we; but leh murder start an' you cahn fine
a man to hole up de side.'[74]

What does this say about the West Indian psyche? One may
say that there are no loyalties because there really is no genuine
sense of unity and that when all is said and done individualism
runs rampant. Some may even suggest a lack of discipline or
an 'excitability,' which precludes the ability to deal with stress,
'a certain psychic tension' which finds relief in laughter and a
shrug of the shoulder.

Brathwaite's compassionate satire 'Ancestors' says so much,
illuminates so gently the dilemma of the West Indian that it
needs no elaboration. This West Indian is a lot more complex
a figure than a simple label like 'Mimic Men' can ever hope to
explain.

Ancestors

'Every Friday morning my grandfather
left his farm of canefields, chickens, cows
and rattled in his trap down to the harbour town
to sell his meat. He was a butcher,
Six-foot-three and very neat: high collar
winged with a grey cravat, a waist coat, watch

chain just above the belt, thin narrow-
bottomed trousers, and the shoes his wife
would polish every night. He drove the trap
himself: slap of the leather reins
along the horse's back and he'd be off
with a top-hearted homburg on his head.
Black English country gentleman.'[75]

The theme of creative imagination recurs for Brathwaite
in the form of possession and a return to latent powers—
the metaphor—'the word becomes again a god and walks
among us.' The veve marks which start a vodoun ceremony
are themselves symbols just as words are symbols. Ogun is
the Yoruba and Afro Caribbean creator God. Seen as divine
craftsman, these sources must be tapped in order to create.

To sum up, Brathwaite looks at the Afro Caribbean man
through his journeys, exile, migrations, his dance, his music,
his worship. He probes the psyche of the West Indian and
recognises his complexity, his resilience and his creativity.
Brathwaite implies that integration and wholeness are
possible when there is acceptance by the Afro-West Indian of
his African past. With this acceptance he can genuinely be a
new man in the New World. From this feeling of rootedness,
identity can now be forged and something torn and new
created.[76]

Yet the pursuit of an African past may remain a metaphysical
abstraction unless there is also a concrete possession by
African people in the Caribbean of the landscape which their
labour has transformed. Such a metaphysic, which is not
rooted in a base material achievement, becomes a form of

cultural therapy in lieu of full healing.

This question of labour possessing the landscape it has transformed offers a possibility of genuine cultural wealth, and raises the formidable challenge of the Indian presence in the making of the Caribbean house. They have been an equally potent force of labour. It is their common/similar relation to production which gives African and Indian equal claim to the landscape as both shared in a common culture of labour and in almost identical circumstances of political and economic organization. It is this reality which frightened the colonial masters and continues to frighten the new indigenous ruling classes in both Guyana and Trinidad. With the exception of *Of Age and Innocence*,[77] I know of no Caribbean prose fiction that has been influenced and informed by a vision of this possibility. But it is at the centre of the early Martin Carter.[78]

Three

Wilson Harris and Character Fulfilment

Harris' concern with the metaphor of the 'melting pot', his insistence on the futility of pursuing concepts of racial inferiority/superiority, spring from his awareness of 'the violent mixture of races that has bred him,' not the least of which was Amerindian. He is no less a victim of the unpleasant beginnings of his history than any other Caribbean writer. He, too, has tried to confront the irrational features which lie under the ground of our collective experience in racial terms.

The stresses of the social context have been looked at squarely in an effort to penetrate the self deceptions, the prejudices and customs and to create something from the void. Harris is aware of the damaged psyche which is a result of the rejection of the 'African Cargo' and conversely he is aware of the danger of making an 'unqualified embrace' of the African as opposed to any other ethnic group. His movement to wholeness is seen in alchemical terms, but it is clear that his alchemy has more to do with unconscious acceptance of the denied, inner self.

It is Harris' faith that the damaged psyche can be restored, not through flight, exile or isolation but by embracing the dark side of human nature without shame, fear or guilt.

> 'What in my view is remarkable about the West Indian in depth is a sense of subtle links, the series of subtle and nebulous links which are latent within him, the latent ground of old and new personalities. This is a very difficult view to hold, I grant because it is not a view which consolidates, which invests in any way in the consolidation of popular character. Rather it seeks to visualise a fulfilment of character.'[79]

I particularly wish to address myself to examining Wilson Harris' pursuit of the goal of 'fulfilment of character'. What is implied in this approach is that the 'interior spaces' of man, the whole comedy of the psyche rather than situation is to be explored. This he sees as consistent with the native tradition 'the depth of inarticulate feeling and unrealized well of emotion belonging to the whole West Indies.' [80]

It is safe to say that Harris is the West Indian *par excellence*, in that his central concern is the exploration of the psyche of West Indian man. Harris rejects the notion of consolidation of character or consolidation of situations since he thinks it tends to simplify experience. What exactly would he choose to consolidate in the Caribbean? How can one seriously consider consolidation of classes and vested interests in the flux that is Caribbean society? Can this be done by inauthentic people? Can this be done by people who are 'imprisoned' by history?

'Within each prisoner of history is an attachment, involuntary perhaps but concrete, to the very premises of his age. How could it be otherwise when those premises are all he possesses or is possessed by.'[81]

At the centre of his work is the juxtaposition of the immensity and power of the universe with 'this cosmic frailty' (which is man). His orientation then would lead to a conception of the novel to fit the perceived needs of the artist. What this means is the creation of a novel which is West Indian rather than English or Russian a unique creation—which in plumbing the psyche of West Indian man argues at insights which are applicable to the family of man.

But Harris' concern is with the potential of man for good or evil, and always there is the question of choice.

'Yet this cosmic frailty (which is man) brings a terrifying authority into human affairs, into the structure of civilization in terms of understanding and protection, or in terms of anguish and exposure depending on the kind of world we build, the kind of living substance we realise and cherish, or the kind of dominating spirit of god we set up to chastise us.'[82]

Thus if we are to choose the kind of world we build and to make a choice we can live with, we must plumb those 'nebulous links which are latent within us'. This descent into the unconscious is fraught with dire consequences, sometimes frightening, sometimes painful, sometimes dangerous. It could lead to schizophrenia, but the descent is necessary for fulfilment and authenticity's sake.

The purpose of the descent as universally exemplified in the myth of the hero is to show that only in the region of danger (watery abyss, cavern, forest island, cattle etc.) can one find the treasure hard to attain jewel, virgin, life potion, victory over death).'[83]

One of the most difficult treasures for the individual to attain, it would seem, is true freedom. The idea of freedom in Harris' novel, I venture to say, is intimately bound up with political implications for West Indian man. I hope to show some relationship between Harris' concept of the novel and his not so obvious political position. Of the few West Indians who have read Wilson Harris, a disproportionate number have accused Harris of being somehow apolitical. The more I have read Harris' novels and the more I have tried to follow what he says about his work and his philosophy, the more I have become convinced that the people who have spoken of Harris' apolitical stance were probably looking for the wrong thing in his works.

Two quotations throw some light on this:

'Facism (and all that that has come to imply in rigged elections etc.) is a disaster in the Third World, as anywhere else, and makes all the more imperative the growth of a body of criticism in dialogue with the nature of freedom.'[84]

and

'That eclipse may effectively conceal not only the reality of the past but the inner, the naked terrifying reality of the present and take away the burden of confrontation with the unpleasant beginnings indeed savaged gift of life. And yet without such a confrontation there can be no deep-seated re-creative transformation of the problematic present into a future that is more consistent with a genuine response to the miracle of life, and one's society begins to consent more and more nihilistically to collectivist (as well as latent totalitarian) premises.'[85]

C.L.R James, I think, has made a very interesting observation when he says that the Promethean individual in literature is disappearing. In his analysis of Melville's Ahab he says:

> 'Ahab is the race of Prometheus. But it seems as if for Melville that type was doomed. Great men, leading their fellows from one stage of civilization to another there have always been and will always be, but the Promethean individual containing in himself, his ideas, his plans, the chart of the future, he seems finished. In the world of affairs he leads only to disaster, that is why perhaps in literature he no longer appears at all.' [86]

James had observed that Prometheus was the 'prototype of the revolutionary leader, benefactor of humanity, bold, defiant, confident.' For those who felt that West Indian literature had to be a literature of protest with facile solutions for the problems of West Indian man, what Harris was saying just did not seem to mean anything. Yet Harris has asked if freedom devoid of original vision can signify anything 'other than incessant protest, political ornament, nationalist and collectivist propaganda, as given code given costume of colonial societies?[87] He answers thus:

> 'The complex task of unraveling those codes is a major exercise of the creative imagination that is central to our age in the continuing development of literature, whether

that development arises 'at home' or abroad.' [88]

This is a difficult impasse for zealous students to overcome since it may serve their own 'humanist' purpose to insist on protest as realism, to institutionalize a species of reportage as the total function of colonial or post colonial literatures.

Not for Harris, the role of strident protester: he sets himself the Penelopean task of unravelling the 'given codes' of the society. To come to terms with the nature of freedom, one has to come to terms with and confront all the conflicts within the West Indian personality. Harris, in rejecting the 'comedy of manners,' where there is a certain code of reason which operates and where one analyses behaviour in terms of what is apparently just for what Harris terms 'the comedy of psyche' you have to pay much closer attention to all sorts of irrational features which lie under the Caribbean man's ground of experience? Unless these features are unearthed the psyche of the West Indian would make him easy prey to collective and totalitarian premises.'

C.L.R. James, in discussing the 'good life', makes the point that all development takes place as a result of self-movement, not organization or direction of external forces, and that we have alien powers within ourselves to overcome. He rejected the notion that raising the standard of living was a solution. 'Men are not pigs to be fattened.'[89] Harris says:

'the 'creative worker' at whom we have been looking—
both transcends and undermines (or deepens if you will)
the mode of society since the truth of community which
he pursues is not a self-evident fact: It is neither purely
circumscribed by nor purely produced by economic

47

circumstance. To put it another way – the so-called economic unity of man (the storyline of progress) is an illusion, in particular when it is maintained as a blanket moral proposition over the actual and obscure moral crises in the heart of those it professes to change.'[90]

James went on to summarise his theory of development thus:

'a) All development takes place as a result of self-movement, not organization or direction by external forces.

b) Self-government springs from and in the overcoming of antagonisms within an organism, not the struggle against external forces.

c) It is not the world of nature that confronts man as an alien power to overcome. It is the alien power that he has himself created.'[91]

Harris says something similar, he urges that we recognise these powers within ourselves, that we 'retrieve' them before we can truly grow and develop.

'In some degree.... we need to retrieve or bring those 'monsters' back into ourselves, as native to psyche, native to quest for unity through contrasting elements, through the ceaseless tasks of the creative imagination to digest and liberate contrasting spaces rather than succumb to implacable polarisation. Such retrieval is vision.'[92]

Harris' words would remain apt in terms of the changing conditions of the Caribbean as time goes by. For his insistence on fashioning a new consciousness on vision, his use of terms such as 'seeing eye', 'blind eye', 'foresight', 'lighting up', 'awareness', all seem to indicate that 'where there is no vision the people perish'. Or another old song 'there's none so blind as he who would not see' comes to mind. We need to be constantly reminded that our destiny is tied up with our willingness to let go of sacred 'fossils' like Ethnicity, Native land, History, Exploitativeness, Self-will, Self-delusion.

The goal is to strive towards authenticity or wholeness. It is only the authentic person who is truly free. Freedom is the only guarantee against acceptance by victim peoples of themselves as ritual guests of the gods, or of the politicians or intellectuals for that matter.

James is wary of the totalitarian personality whether he be politician or intellectual. In his analysis of Melville's *Ishamel* he says:

> 'Thus, the totalitarian personality devoid of human feeling and restraint; no longer the master, but the instrument of his purpose embodies in action, the theoretical conclusions of the disoriented intellectual. No wonder that, with terror in his soul, Ishmael follows Ahab as the guilt ridden intellectual of today often with some terror finds refuge in the idea of the one party totalitarian state.'[93]

But James thinks the artist in the society must exercise an influence on it. Harris extends our vision, our consciousness as he should:

> 'A supreme artist exercises an influence on the national consciousness which is incalculable. He is created by it, but he himself illuminates and amplifies it, bringing the

past up to date and charting the future. We tend to accept this in general.'[94]

Harris' view of fiction is that it is a tool to liberate consciousness from the imaginative straightjacket of social form. In this way we perceive ourselves and conditions differently and may then use more strategies towards coping with reality.

> 'A major task of creativity is to penetrate complex self-deceptions as well as the complex values with which we have invested objects or orders that we have come to take for granted. There are two ways in which it is possible to react to this penetration or erosion of values. One is by submitting to it as absolute loss or oppression as the pre-Columbian peoples submitted to the Spanish conquerors. The other is by anticipating in the logic of creative imagination, an exposure of involuntary codes by which we are conscripted and therefore digesting by degrees a state of change, which left to its own natural or unnatural devices would overwhelm us in the long run. This is the role of the physical arrow which involves an involuntary break through of prejudices and Customs.'[95]

This long quotation from the essay Animism/Realism, by Peterson and Rutherford underscores Harris' concern with self-deceptions, but lest we meet the fate of pre-Columbian peoples, we should begin to expose those codes, those fetishes which have stamped us as West Indians and break through to freedom by digesting change. To be fascinated by a sense of loss whether of history or place, and to wallow in feelings of oppression prepare the climate for conquest, and conquest after Columbus is mainly for us, a conquest of our minds which leads us to become either helpless and futile passive reactors, rather than, active, creative purposeful makers of a just world.

The idea of history in the Caribbean as something we have or have not; the idea of culture of tradition as something we borrow or have not; any of the 'fossils' we perceive ourselves by, are seen not as reason for a questionable sense of inferiority, but freshly interpreted, can be an opportunity to create something form this void.

'The survivors—a long and precarious line extending into the twentieth century—possess all the symptoms of 'historylessness' rootlessness – stigmata of the void.

This need not be, I feel a totally disabling fact or feature in fact, it may constitute a most fruitful obsession, an obsession with an art of compassion, a continuous salvage of vessels of sensibility between man and man, and man and nature – a salvage which seeks never to block its own agencies of vision of idolatrous fixations.'[96]

Those who have wrestled with the problem of history as a medium of documentation of man's existence have begun to feel that this approach is probably not as useful as the creative artist's approach in terms of making statements about what is permanent and lasting about human life.

'Hence the partial justification of those who, like, Charles Peguy in his Clio, have accused history of an inevitable blindness to the mutual impingement and attraction of what is timeless, and of what is most obviously temporal, because most particular, most chancy, most growing in human life, poetry in its great classic forms was evidently far better suited that is history, to emphasize these aspects of life.'[97]

Harris rejects the complacent native land 'fetish' if one is to be truly free.

> 'The education of freedom (and you have been one of my unconscious tutors in whom and with whom I grew into the heart of 'negative' identity, self-contradiction, even 'positive' loathing of the 'ground' of spirit) begins with a confession of the need to lose the base concretion men seek to impose when they talk of one's 'native' land (or another's) as if it were fixed and anchored in place. In this age and time, one's native land (and the other's) is always crumbling. Crumbling with a capacity of vision which rediscovers the process to be not foul and destructive but actually the constructive secret of all creation, wherever one happens to be.'[98]

In the face of so much that is insular, parochial and limited, an idea like this would encourage change in a society which always seems to give lip service to unity and community. Nothing is created without something being destroyed. All creation has to do with birth/death, beginnings/endings. Change is inevitable; something new is created every time old structures crumble – if even it is desolation which is left behind.

What Harris' vision is, is essentially a Caribbean man, who has freed himself from his 'irrationalities' by retrieving the 'monsters' and confronting them, thereby loosening the hold they have on him.

> '....so eternity to season
> the barbaric conflict of man
> so he must die first to be free.'[99]

This new freedom could well prepare him to fully participate in his own destiny in an authentic way. We still have the freedom of choice, which could sensibly be pursued by free men. I see what Harris is doing in literature as complementing Jacques Monod's vision for man.

Monod says,

> 'Where then shall we find the source of truth and the moral inspiration for a really scientific socialist humanism? Only we suggest in the sources of science itself, in the ethic upon which knowledge is founded and which by free choice makes knowledge the supreme value – the measure and guarantee for all other values. An ethic which bases moral responsibility upon the very freedom of that axiomatic choice.'[100]

Monod has, in common with Wilson Harris, the desire for men to be authentic and asserts that his authenticity can only be achieved by freeing himself from the 'misleading servitudes of animism.'

> 'Harris argued along the same lines and said that to overlook the nature of realism as complex as imbued with many levels from the past, that determine our way of seeing, thinking, feeling is to succumb to animism as realism.'[101]

We can see Harris now not in any simple sense of the word as political, rather for those whose 'seeing eye' is limited, those whose vision is blurred by 'irrationalities' he is apolitical, but he is not so much apolitical as beyond politics in its most limited sense. Harris' attempt, though it might appear political, is connected with Caribbean man's need to establish a basic identity from which wholeness can grow, since Caribbean peoples' political commitment is tightly linked to the concept of the split person. His is the role of the visionary, the prophet, the guide who sees the need for a 'supplement of soul' in man. At least, one critic sees him in this role. In her essay 'Tumatumari and the Imagination of Wilson Harris,' Joyce Adler speaks of Harris' 'commitment to man.' But quotes from the physicist De Broglie and says it seems to apply to this work.

> 'Often the feeling of the imminence of a danger gives birth in the heart of men to sentiments.... Which can serve to avoid it ... confronted by dangers... man has need of a supplement of soul and he must force himself to acquire it promptly before it is too late. It is the duty of those who have the mission of being the spiritual or intellectual guides of humanity to labour to awaken in it this supplement of soul.'[102]

By reference to Harris' novels, I would like to pinpoint what he has to say about the following irrationalities:

(a) Ethnicity and Negative identity
(b) Exploitativeness
(c) History
(d) Self-will or will to power (the Promethean character)
(e) Attitudes to women

There is a sense in which some of these headings overlap. For example, one finds that when Harris illustrates through his novels his views on Ethnicity and Negative Identity, it bears upon what he thinks of History or Exploitativeness. I will none-the-less start with Ethnicity and Negative Identity.

'It meant rallying of all their forces into an incestuous persona and image an alliance—the very antithesis of their dark truth and history written in the violent mixture of races that has bred them as though their true mother was a wanton on the face of the earth and their true father a vagrant and a rogue from every continent.'[103]

Kenneth Ramchand states that Harris 'issues a warning' (which is implicit in all his writings) against the construing of any racial heritage in the Caribbean as either model or crucible for the future.[104]

Harris seems to be at pains to show the 'violent mixture of races' in his characters. If we take a sample of the racial mix of some of his characters, we see an interesting array of ethnic variety.

'He has never known his father who had been in his middle fifties (his mother being at the time in her late thirties) when he was born. Soon after his father died suddenly. His mother possessed a very good snapshot, it had acquired a sub-aqueous background look over the years, but still revealed a dark big man of vivid African descent. His mother on the other hand was a delicate, almost aerial figure of a woman, half French, half English. Her skin was like a fair East Indian's shadowed by night-black wings of hair. It was rumoured that along with her European stock, she possessed a fraction of Amerindian blood as well, and that her grandmother was Arawak as her husband's grandfather had been uncompromisingly

African.'[105]

'Mattias Gomes, a Portuguese/Assyrian merchant of the Pomeron. Cameron's great grandfather had been a dour Scot, and his great grandmother an African slave and mistress. Cameron was related to Schomburgh (whom he addressed as Uncle with the other members of the crew) and it was well known that Schomburgh's great grandfather was an Arawak American Indian. The whole crew was one spiritual family living and dying together in a common grave out of which they had sprung again from the same soul and womb as it were. They were all knotted and bound together in the enormous bruised head of Cameron's ancestry and nature as in the white unshaven head of Schomburgh's age and presence.'[106]

'He was Eurasian (Amerindian on the wrong side of the blanket) and though he never directly confessed it, afraid of his African cargo, African momentum, African legacy.'[107]

'Da Silva da Silva was born in Brazil of Spanish and Portuguese parents, invisible black antecedents as well, seminal shadows they seemed in the madonna pool extending up into the Andes where fire was snow.'[108]

What is Harris saying to us, by giving these detailed genealogies? We have noted previously the psychological effects of Caribbean man's acceptance of a racial hierarchy. These obsessions with racial inferiority or superiority led to the denial of much that was truly creative. The denied part of the individual struggled for recognition in psychologically unhealthy ways. This dark and unrecognised side of the human person suppressed, led to the 'scarecrow' existence of

Henry Tenby whose skeleton in the cupboard was his 'African Cargo'.

'Henry Tenby had become his own prisoner, sterile and inauthentic. He was victim of history. It is useless to deny it. Prudence's father wrote on the diary of the well (which death had overridden and which he had been unable to destroy man lives in history and it will take centuries—whatever mask of emancipation he wears—it will take perhaps another thousand years of flight through space for him to emerge from the psychology of fear. To descend into himself as into all men.'[109]

It was Henry Tenby's fate to accept such a hopeless fate for himself. Had he another view of history might he not have been a fully integrated whole person?

'What about fertility? I asked, what about the imaginative cultivation of certain truths as far as we can discern them in the river of time, that changes its bed, that meanders.'[110]

Prudence his daughter, can move from breakdown to wholeness, but to do this she had to confront her 'history.'

'Take the game I have been playing' Prudence wrote addressing the cradle of the waterfall. I call it the game of inner space, at first I assure myself it was nothing–a trick of exploitation, a fantasy–nothing more. I would wake up normal as punch the morning after the night before. But then suddenly—it is difficult to explain—the game had become real. Real as hell is real, believe me. No umbrella could stave off such a deluge. All the idols in the world were raining cats and dogs, rainfall of idolatries, splintering of perfectionist assumptions, I had never dreamt to question. I was stunned by their fall, the fall of the city of fold, fall of Eldorado, fall of the cliff of faith (to which I still cling as if it were Roi's scaffold); fall of the nonreciprocal statue of love (carbon dioxide upon Venus), fall of the nonreciprocal glory of war (brick in the head of Mars). And as these models crumbled it began to dawn upon me that a new spatial womb existed whose reciprocal functions one had long denied—new engines or structures of the psyche—stone woman of Tumaturari at the ringside of history (translation of the Gorgan – incredible as it may seem – into enduring compassion) woman of the scaffold beneath the slave of Canje (translation of the Gorgan incredible as the association seems into the cap of love); woman of poverty – Mahaicony and Abary (translation of the Gorgan – strange as it appears – into the queen of necessity).'[111]

All idolatries whether they be of wealth, faith, love or war must be taken from the pedestals, we put them on, in order to become compassionate, loving and truly free persons.

While Henry Tenby is afraid of his 'African cargo' and does not confront it, to his loss; Harris does not advocate an unqualified embracing of the African, as opposed to any other ethnic group. For him, it is important not to exploit this particular aspect of Caribbean man's history or any other.

Fenwick, in *Secret Ladder*, is aware of the possibilities of this meeting with Poseidon, 'the black man with the European name'.

'I wish I could truly grasp the importance of this meeting.

If I do not – if my generation do not – leviathan will swallow us all. It isn't a question of fear – it's a question of going in unashamed to come out of the womb again.

I am not being political. Far from it. The issue for me is fundamental and psychological. It is the real issue of genuine and worthwhile authority. To misconceive the African, I believe, if I may use such an expression as misconceive at this stage, is to misunderstand and exploit him mercilessly and oneself as well. For there in this creature Poseidon, the black man with the European name drawn out of the depths of time, is the emotional dynamic of liberation that happened a century and a quarter ago – to put a rough date on it.

Something went tragically wrong then. Something was misunderstood and frustrated. God alone knows why and how. Like an affair between a man and a woman gone wrong. Maybe it was all too emotional, too blinding, this freedom that has turned cruel abortive, evasive, woolly and wild everywhere almost. And yet the affair is still fresh in our mind, and so it is not really finished.'[112]

Harris' concern with the twin questions of freedom and authority are examined in this book and underscore my contention, that for Harris, the creative imagination of the Caribbean artist must be put to use in the cause of genuine freedom of the Caribbean man. Any narrow political propagandising simply tightens the limiting and limited vision which we may choose to accept in terms of our history, and in the same way our social behaviour might be schizoid simply because we have accepted the prison of history.

Poseidon is symbolic of that freedom 'that has turned

cruel, abortive, evasive woolly and wild everywhere almost.' Poseidon's grandfather has been a runaway slave, and some people believed that Poseidon was a hundred years old, hounded by his grandfather's crazed spirit. Poseidon is not only the inheritor of a 'free spirit', but the living example of a man who did not have to await the indignity of 'emancipation' the official stamp put on a disgraceful period of imperialist history in the Caribbean, for the very good reason that it no longer made economic sense to carry the burden of slavery in these parts.

What went wrong then? What was misunderstood and frustrated in this experiment in freedom? Was there any fundamental change in the attitudes of master and slave to each other? Did either conceive of the other's humanity in a new light? Was there a genuine recognition that something significant has been hoped for in terms of human destiny? Was it only an exercise in bitterness, revenge and recrimination?

The objective circumstances which created Poseidon's grandfather's action are no longer the same circumstances which obtain for Poseidon; since Poseidon shall we say, underwent a 'river change' when he was born to free parents rather than slaves, but it does not seem as though Poseidon has moved beyond the particular psychological framework of 'runaway slave' which not only keeps him riveted to one spot, but makes him completely vulnerable and distrustful of change.

Poseidon is blind to the disintegration of both his physical surroundings (the house) or his personality. Fear of change, fear of the inroads of 'science', fear of genuine confrontation, inability to face up to these fears, to open up to the truth

60

of present reality would lead to the death of Poseidon—the death of a conception of freedom, for truly freedom is so much more than flight, exile or isolation.

At one point in time, it seemed so right, so correct for Poseidon's grandfather to have escaped from slavery, that particular reality, that denial of a man's humanity, but unless we romanticise Poseidon's present condition, and turn a blind eye on reality, we cannot but see that Poseidon has not gone beyond his grandfather, as a matter of fact, he has regressed, for given his grandfather's spirit, and had he returned to the here and now, his bid for freedom may have taken more progressive directions in keeping with the times.

'I am glad we can see him as he is so that we can know what this life is, the hard business of this life, here and now (do you follow me) and indeed we can see –beyond a shadow of – doubt the necessity for human freedom.'[113]

Let us look at Poseidon's house as a symbol of Poseidon's dilemma. The house 'was one of the most solid (though disintegrating) houses in the canje'.

'That house was built on solid premises at one point in time. One's eyes were drawn back compulsively to the exotic mission house created equally by destiny and accident and Fenwick experienced a peculiar thrill as if he were witnessing a curious historic question of fact. To what and whose spirit did the house belong? Had it been grafted from above (unconscious of itself) on to the land, or did it possess a self conscious kinship and identity beneath. It had an air both foreign and native, ideal and primitive, at one and the same time, and yet it seems so precariously and absolutely right, belonging so truly in this natural or unnatural context of landscape, that the thought of an imposition of pretentiousness or absurdity in the life of the crumbling building, seemed equally ridiculous and impossible. In fact – if it has been the gift of an imposing high divinity – it bore a certain generous conception, economic and still humane. There were no marks of exclusiveness – rather a spirit of all inclusive privacy, the most welcome artifice of humanity.

What was at stake here was not the inevitable ruin of an old house, but a perception of depth more lasting than time, the moral privilege and right of place. This was Poseidon's asylum and home. It has acquired a special seal and privilege, the stamp of a multiple tradition or heritage. If he did not want to abandon the place, who and what could compel him to leave at this stage, save brute force? Had he not the right to defy all the sciences of the earth, in the blessed name of his humanity?'[114]

It is precisely this 'multiple tradition or heritage' which is the strength of Caribbean people, it is this eclecticism which Harris associates with our strength, but the normal advances of civilization are also part of this 'multiple tradition' which we should embrace, but to glorify or romanticise primitivism or poverty is to deny ourselves a vital role in the development of man. Primitive yes; subservience to degradation, no.

'Maybe that is why Poseidon is a God, after all' Fenwick thinks. He teaches us the terrifying depth of our human allegiance, our guilt in the fact of humanity, our subservience to the human condition. But he cannot force us surely, to make an idol of this present degrading form.'[115]

Poseidon's attempt now to reject 'science', to fail to embrace an opportunity for the normal advancement of civilization is to betray his grandfather's spirit and signals the end of an era and the beginning of another.

Not only does the African presence need to be scrutinized in the light of twentieth century realities, but Harris is understandably committed to examining the implications for Guyana in particular of the native Amerindians' nebulous position in present day Guyana. The Amerindian woman in Harris' novels invariably represent the folk—the idea of the folk, the folk consciousness, which seems as elusive as the Petras, Mariellas and Rakkas who seem to be not only the rocks on which a people's fate is built, but guides into the unknown terrain of the physical interior of Guyana and the psychological inner spaces of Promethan characters like Donne of Palace of the Peacock.

Michael Gilkes makes the cogent observation:

> 'Petra is a composite figure who also embodies Mariella of Palace of the Peacock (1960). In Heartland, having returned to her people pregnant with Donne (or da Silva's) child, she is banished to Kartabo Point. This is of course a significant locale. The home of Mittelholzer's Kaywana and the source of the Van Groenwegel family tree. It is noteworthy, however, that Harris sees the locale as a starting point for the birth of a creative, rather than divided racial consciousness. He quotes from Harris:

> 'It was at Kartabo Point that one found the beginnings of a new legendary continental offspring born of many races.' [116]

It is remarkable that Harris seems to have escaped the Caribbean man's malaise of being unable to positively assess the woman, the feminine principle in the Caribbean. His depiction of women is usually associated with strength, with the ability to firmly grasp reality; their feet are invariably bare, grasping the ground.

'Her feet were bare and covered in red dust from the public road. Her legs were heavily made, powerfully and beautifully drawn within the loose dress she wore. She seemed immovable, rough and tender, riveted into a dance of unconscious sex, unconscious passivity grounded in activity as he stood by the sea wall. Moseley opened the dish she brought to him; and ate a hunk of bread with a slice of fish.[117]

It enfolded her making her look like a queen wishing to make a magnificent and enigmatic gift of herself to a hungry crowd, the more mysterious because gratuitous and barbaric, the column of her neck and her arms were bare, and her naked feet were planted squarely on the ground.'[118]

It is interesting that the schizophrenic is usually associated with flight, with an inability to be 'grounded' and that this particular insight of Harris,' that women's strength and guidance must be recognised and accepted for what it is worth by Caribbean man in order for them to experience this wholeness, this vision of 'cauda pavonis'. Harris' novels are essentially dramas of the unconscious processes and he uses the vocabulary and images of alchemy. It is necessary to quote from alchemical literature to understand Harris' metaphors for he uses the concepts of alchemy. Harris sees human beings moving through processes of transmutation, moving through stages, from darkness and confusion to light, ignorance to understanding, division to wholeness.

'The nigredo or blackness (fig 115) is in the initial state either present from the beginning as a quality of the prima materia, the chaos or massa confusa, or else produced by the separation (solutio, speartio, diviso, putrefactio) of the elements. If the separated condition is assumed at the start, as sometimes happens then a union of opposites is performed in the likeness of a male and female (called the coniugium, matrimonium, coniunctio, coitus) followed by the death of the product of the union (mortificatio, calcinatio, putrefacto) and a corresponding nigredo. From this, the washing (ablutio, baptisma) either leads direct to the whitening (albedo) or else the soul (anima) released and the 'death' is reunited with the dead body and brings about its resurrection or finally the many colours (onmes calores) or 'peacock's tail' colours. At this point the first main goal of the process is reached, namely the albedo, tinctura alba, terra alba foliata, lapis albus etc., highly prized by many alchemists as if it were the ultimate goal.'[119]

What does this all add up to? Carl Jung states quite categorically that alchemy had more to do with unconscious processes than any real faith of the alchemist in producing gold, since so little was produced (even this is questionable) for so much expenditure of time and devotion.

'Alchemy sets itself the task of acquiring this 'treasure hard to attain' and of producing it in visible form, as physical gold or the panacea or the transforming tincture – in so far as the art still buried itself in the laboratory.

But in so far as the practical chemical work was never quite free from the unconscious contents of the operator which found expression in it, it was at the same time a psychic activity, which can best be compared with what we call active imagination.

This enables us to get an active grasp of things that also find expression in dream life. The process is in both cases an irrigation of the conscious mind by the unconscious, and it is so closely related to the world of alchemical ideas, that we are probably justified in assuming that alchemy deals with the same, or very similar processes as those involved in active imagination and dreams ultimately with the process of individuation.'[120]

Whether we choose to view Harris' women as women or as the soul or anima, the sub-conscious of Caribbean man, Harris advises that we accept women's roles, embrace them rather than be ashamed of them.

'Then stop feeling eternal shame about me and you Abram. I is you body-in-the-dark woman, you convenient sphinx of a woman. She laughed, I's feel you standing far away upon some high spirit–branch like a bird falling every now and then to pick a blind red pepper.'[121]

It is this sense of disassociation, of unacknowledgement by the individual of this 'body-in-the-dark'. The dark side of his nature which Harris is appealing to us to accept without shame, to do so is to attain the integrity of self and wholeness of the divided person. And this brings us to the self-will or will to power, which we must also see as negative features of our society.

Donne's desire to dominate others and exploit them creates a wall, which further divides him from the folk whose community of interests and insights, as a figure of authority he ought to embrace. This model of authority is destructive of the humanity of people.

> 'Dreamer', he warned, giving me a light wooden tap on the shoulder. 'Life here is tough.' One has to be a devil to survive. I'm the last landlord. I tell you. I fight everything in nature, flood, drought, chicken hawk, rat beast and woman. I'm everything. Midwife, yes doctor, yes; gaoler, judge, hangman, every blasted thing to the labouring people. Look man, look outside again Primitive. Every boundary line is a myth. No man's land, understand?'[122]

What C.L.R. James sees as the cause of the division between Ishmael and the crew of Melville's, Moby Dick is applicable to Donne's situation.

> 'What keeps them apart is his intellectualism, his inability to embrace reality spontaneously, the doubt and fear and guilt and isolation from people, which compel him at all times to seek to find out what is happening to himself in relation to the world.'[123]

There is a sense in which Donne's development is arrested in the same way he arrests "Mariella" and ill-treats her – this desire to dominate nature rather than to live in harmony with nature diminished him. This Donne himself recognises.

> I am beginning to lose all my imagination save that sometimes I feel I'm involved in the most frightful material slavery. I hate myself sometimes, hate myself for being the most violent taskmaster—I drive myself

with no hope of redemption whatsoever and I lash the folk.'[124]

Slowly but surely enlightemnent dawns on Donne, he realises that he must have a different relationship with the folk, and this can only come through love not self-will.

'A singular thought always secured him to the scaffolding. It was the unflinching clarity with which he looked into himself and saw that all his life he had loved no one but himself. He focussed his blind eye with all penitent might on his pinpoint star and reflection as one looking into the void of oneself upon far greater love and self-protection that have made the universe.'[125]

He finds fulfilment at last in the realization that neither through fear nor will power, neither through cruelty nor pride can wholeness come. The other, and the otherness of our being must be embraced with love before we can hear the music of the spheres and dance in harmony with our true nature.

One was what I am in the music – buoyed and supported above dreams by the undivided soul and anima in the universe from whom the word of dance and creation first came. The command, to the starred peacock who was instantly transposed to know and to hug himself his true, invisible otherness and opposition, his true alien spiritual love without cruelty and confusion in the blindness and frustration of desire. It was the dance of all fulfilment I now held and knew deeply, cancelling my forgotten fear of strangeness and catastrophe in a destitute world.'[126]

Harris's insistence on the wholeness of man is evidenced

by his commitment to confronting the hidden and buried consciousness, he believes that it is only by this effort can integrity of self be attained.

Four

Naipaul's Dilemma

'So writing, for all its initial
distorting clarifies and even
becomes a process of life'

VS. Naipaul, Mimic Men

Walcott talks of his schizophrenia in terms of black and white.

'That wrestling contradiction of being white in mind and black in body as if the flesh were coal from which the spirit like tormented smoke writhed to escape.'[127]

And in the colonial' attitude to his coloniser's culture:

'The pride of the colonial in the culture of his mother country was fiercer than her true children's because the colonial feared to lose her.'[128]

Naipaul's predicament is more complex, he is in a double bind as an ex-colonial and an East Indian who grew up insulated from the wider creole society by the Hindu-Brahmin world of his clan. His avowed distaste for the place of his birth (Trinidad) and his rather ambivalent attitude toward black people, bind him in curious ways to his vision of Caribbean life and manners as barren and destructive of what is highest and noblest in man.

In a Free State, is a good starting point to look at Naipaul's dilemma. The question of freedom is examined episodically. One is constantly on the move as it were, as though freedom and escape are synonymous. A journey is not entirely a question of space, distance or place. A journey may also be an adventure into oneself, it could be a journey towards the most meaningful quest an individual can make—knowledge of self.

'Does The Tramp at Piraeus see himself as a free man? I've been to Egypt six or seven times. Gone around the world about a dozen times. Australia, Canada, all those countries. Geologist, or used to be. First went to Canada in 1923, Been there about eight times now. I've been travelling for thirty eight years. Youth hostelling that's how I do it. Not a thing to be despised. New Zealand, have you been there? I went there in 1934. Between you and me they're a cut above the Australians. But what's nationality these days? I myself I think of myself as a citizen of the world.'[129]

Naipaul describes his speech as one of dates, places and numbers. The tramp was a lonely isolated, human being who knew 'he was odd'. But he might have believed that he was free. This brings one to the real question: of what does freedom consist? Surely if it were simply freedom of movement, sheer mobility, it would not occupy anyone's serious attention, particularly not Caribbean writers' attention, since they have been most mobile. William Walsh describes Naipaul:

> 'But Naipaul is also a remarkably free untethered soul, an expatriate in his birth place, an alien in his ancestral land, a disengaged observer of Britain and other countries. Mobility is the breath of life to him.'[130]

It almost sounds like a description of the tramp, and of course I question Walsh's use of the word 'free,' since it seems to imply that freedom is a matter of space, place or distance rather than a state of mind. Erich Fromm in his book. *The Fear of Freedom* notes that while modem man is free from the bonds of pre-individualistic society which, while giving him security limited him, he has not really gained freedom in the positive sense, that is, the full realization of his individual self.

'Positive freedom, consists in the spontaneous activity of the total integrated personality'.[131] He goes on to say that spontaneity has a very important component which is love.

> 'Love is the foremost component of such spontaneity, not love as the dissolution of the self in another person, nor love as the possession of another person, but love as spontaneous affirmation of others, as the union of the individual with others on the basis of the preservation of the individual self. The dynamic quality of love lies in this very polarity; that it springs from the need of overcoming separateness that it leads to oneness – and yet that individuality is not eliminated.'[132]

The whole question of isolation, or the 'overcoming of separateness' is the key to the tramp's dilemma, he is incapable of overcoming his separateness. We are told that the tramp spoke to a Yugoslav, a fellow traveller, but that when the Yugoslav smiled and made interjections, the tramp neither saw nor heard.

> 'He couldn't manage a conversation. He wasn't looking for conversation. He didn't even require an audience. It was as though, over the years, he had developed this way of swiftly explaining himself to himself, reducing his life to names and numbers.'[133]

Naipaul continues by saying,

> 'He hadn't wanted company, he wanted only the camouflage and protection of company.'[134]

Here we have a failure to relate in any genuine, authentic way to another individual—the inability to love, in the sense of recognition and respect for another individual. This total isolation, this fleeing from one place to another, is an extreme form of alienation an inability to root oneself in the world of one's fellow men.

Santosh, in *One Out of Many*, is a pathetic figure. Nothing seems more nihilistic than his definition of what freedom means to him.

> 'Then I looked in the mirror and decided to be free. All that my freedom has brought me is the knowledge that I have a face and have a body. That I must feed this body and clothe this body for a certain number of years. Then

it will be over.'[135]

What exactly is the nature of this freedom? Santosh has been brought to North America from India, a servant of a diplomat. In Bombay he was happy, he knew his place, his life was circumscribed by his caste, his job, his society.

> 'I was so happy in Bombay. I was respected, I had a certain position. I worked for an important man. The highest in the land came to our bachelor chambers and enjoyed my food and showered compliments on me. I also had my friends. We met in the evenings on the pavement below the gallery of our chambers. Some of us like the sailors, bearer and myself, were domestic who lived in the street. The others were people who came to that bit of pavement to sleep. Respectable people, we didn't encourage riff-raff.'[136]

Now in Washington D.C. the capital of the United States he leaves his employer, becomes a cook in a restaurant, discovers that he is no longer free from U.S. immigration authorities, he has become an illegal immigrant. He has run away once, where can he run now? Back to Bombay? No. He is advised by his new employer Priya:

> 'Santosh, you have no problems. Marry the hubshi. That will automatically make you a citizen. Then you will be a free man.'[137]

In light of Santosh's avowed position on the hubshi, this seems to be a life sentence, total imprisonment, rather than freedom.

> 'Dishonoured, I say, and I know that this might seem

strange to people over here, who have permitted the hubshi to settle among them in such large numbers and must therefore esteem them in certain ways. But in our country we frankly do not care for the hubshi. It is written in our books, both holy and not so holy, that it's indecent and wrong for a man of our blood to embrace the hubshi woman. To be dishonoured in this life, to be born a cat or a monkey or a hubshi in the next.'[138]

It takes some time to ascertain that the term 'hubshi' applies to black people. It is noteworthy that Naipaul never uses the term 'black people' in the entire story. I believe Naipaul needed to deal with this problem of the relationship between these two ethnic groups (these after all are the two major ethnic groups of his native land, Trinidad, and he is a member of Santosh's) from as it were a protected stance. It would almost seem as though it would have been too daring on his part to use the term 'negroes' or 'black people'. It is very convenient to have a Bombay servant's language and view point to attack the problem. But indeed it clarifies many things.

We hear what is the official religious attitude to the 'hubshi.' We are never allowed a word from the 'hubshi' woman with whom Santosh intends to imprison himself, we simply have a physical description. Is it possible (as indeed happens) that despite the dishonour, Santosh can only deal with the 'hubshi' on a purely physical level? There is no development, no growth, no change in the hubshi's character. This development we cannot know, but we see Santosh in the process of becoming an individual.

'Once my employer had been to me only a presence. I used to tell him that besides him I was as dirt. It was only a way of talking one of the courtesies of our language but it had something of truth. I meant that he was the man who adventured in the world for me that I experienced the world through him, that I was content to be a small part of his presence.'[139]

Santosh continues with something of the guilt of Adam.

'Now I found that, without wishing it, I was ceasing to see myself as part of my employer's presence and beginning at the same time to see him as an outsider might see him, as perhaps the people who came to dinner in the apartment saw him.'[140]

Santosh begins to see his employer as another individual, he begins to use his critical faculty and yes, to judge him. He hears the American who came to dinner boast to his employer that he had acquired a head of a sculpture from the temple, when he visited India, by paying the guide two dollars for hacking it off and who with all the aplomb of the man who knows everyone's price says:

'If I had a bottle of whisky he would have pulled down the whole temple for me.'[141]

Santosh is disappointed when he realises that his employer is not so much upset by the desecration of the temple he is simply insulted in a personal way. Santosh in consoling him tries to put the burden of the offence on the difference of cultural values.

'Sahib, but we know these people are Franks and barbarians'. 'They are malicious people Santosh. They think that because we are a poor country we are all the same. They think an official in government is just the same as some poor guide scraping together a few rupees to keep body and soul together, poor fellow.'

I saw that he has taken the insult only in a personal way and I was disappointed. I thought he had been thinking of the temple.'[142]

So, Santosh's moral sensibilities are more refined than his employer's, he would not have dared to think this way before the 'other' in the form of a 'hubshi' woman began to look upon him as a person, an attractive one at that. He discovered that he was handsome.

'My face was handsome. I had never thought of myself in this way. I had thought of myself as unnoticeable. With features that served as identification alone.'[143]

Santosh seems to have stunted his growth and development by refusing to make the final leap towards wholeness by entering into the 'others' life in a meaningful way. There are remarkable similarities between Santosh's refusal to enter into another dimension of experience and Singh's in *Mimic Men*. Santosh says:

'But my strength in this house is that I am a stranger. I have closed my mind and heart to the English Language, to newspapers and radio and television, to the pictures of 'hubshi' runners and boxers and musicians on the wall. I also do not want to understand or learn any more.'[144]

This is William Walsh's version of the relationship between

Browne and Singh in *Mimic Men*.

> 'In these circumstances Browne's persona, his status as renegade and romantic, as a radical for whose acknowledged gifts the pattern provided no outlet, and Singh's as the young cultivated millionaire, together made an irresistible combination. They supported one another and appeared as a portent no one could discuss. They supported one another in a more intimate way too. The African with his lacerated and uncertain personality needing alien witness to prove his reality found in the Asiatic, Singh a complete persona and an unfractured psyche. Singh was presented by Browne with a picture of himself which it reassured him to study. Singh was disturbed by the dim knowledge that this involved being.'[145]

And here Walsh takes a direct quote from *Mimic Men*.

> '...Committed to a whole new mythology, dark and alien, committed to a series of interiors, I never wanted to enter. Joe Louis, Haile Selassie, Jesus... The distaste and alarm of boyhood rose up strongly.'[146]

Aside from noting Mr. Walsh's insights into the African and Asiatic psyche (which one gathers that he acquired from reading V.S. Naipaul) one cannot miss the similarities between Santosh's and Singh's attitudes to the 'alien' dark mythologies of black people.

This is revealing. It not only underscores the great humiliation and dishonour which Santosh is prepared to undergo to become a free citizen of the United States, but to see himself as free in this context is to view freedom as, simply, total isolation

78

and alienation. It makes one wonder whether Naipaul's own portrayal of black people has not been influenced by this view. No wonder, one senses that at times Naipaul's satire is a little less than humane.

One critic, A.C. Derrick, says:

'In his satiric presentation of characters Naipaul rarely allows himself to show a humane understanding of their weakness.'[147]

I am prepared to differ with Derrick on one count—that in one book (and this is considered his best by all accounts), *A House for Mr Biswas*, is the exception to this pervasive sense of pitiless satire. Gordon Rohlehr makes the point:

'A House for Mr Biswas is more profound than anything else Naipaul has written because for the first time, he is able to feel his own history not merely as a squalid farce, but as an adventure in sensibility.'[148]

Contrast, however, Naipaul's attitude to the slaves' posturing in *The Loss of El Dorado*.

'The New World as make believe: this Negro fantasy life changed and developed. In Trinidad, an immigrant island, it has become many featured, a dream, beyond labour and more real than labour, of power and pettiness, of titles, flags and uniforms, kings and queens and courtiers. The planter looking at his Negroes and seeing only Negroes he never knew. He might know that certain Negroes dressed up in castoff clothes and received other Negroes, fed and danced and jumped up together; a mimicry in the Negro yards of white entertaining. But he didn't know that

that Negro-carter belonging to Rosette Picton, formerly Smith – now taking on a load from the Port of Spain store of Mr. Rigby, a merchant and Negro-shipper. The planter didn't know that the Negro-carter, an especially stupid Negro, was a king at night with twelve courtiers and a uniform of his own, a black coat with a scarlet-collar, and a green ribbon over one shoulder, a hat with a black cockade.'[149]

So for Santosh or Singh or Naipaul the goal of becoming a free self-determining productive individual could never be achieved unless he can become a well integrated individual, leaving behind the pre-individualistic state of development.

These primary ties block his full human development, they stand in the way of the development of his reason and his critical capacities, they let him recognise himself and others only through the medium of his or their participation in a clan a social, or religious community, and as human being, in other words, they block his development, as a free self-determining productive individual. But although this is one aspect, there is another one. This identity with nature clan, religion gives the individual security. He belongs to, he is rooted in, a structuralized whole in which he has an unquestionable place. He may suffer from hunger or suppression, but he does not suffer from the worst of all pains – complete aloneness and doubt.'[150]

Santosh might have left the clan behind, but unless he can determine for himself a relationship which is one of mutual respect and spontaneity with his 'hubshi' wife, he can spend the rest of his life feeding and clothing his body for 'a certain number of years. Then it will be over.' He might as well consider himself a 'dead man' as the 'I' in *Tell Me Who To Kill*, recognises. 'But now the dead man is me.'" *Tell Me Who To Kill* is a story whose theme is essentially that of the barrenness and unproductiveness of hatred. Dayo is committed to a questionable love for his brother which itself turns to hatred. With such a low self-image, such obvious self-contempt it is quite unlikely that a productive loving relationship can blossom in such soil.

The lack of self-respect precludes any real freedom in terms of developing one's potential, without faith in one's self and in life one encloses oneself in a paranoid world – a world which can only end in self-destruction, hence the amazing insight of the 'I' of *Tell Me Who To Kill*. He is indeed 'a dead man', the antithesis of life and creativity... The problem of freedom is not only a quantitative one, but a qualitative one; that we not only have to preserve and increase the traditional freedom, but that we have to gain a new kind of freedom one which enables us to realize our own individual self, to have faith in this self and in life.[151]

We also need a 'spontaneous affirmation of others.' In other words, positive freedom consists in the spontaneous activity of the total integrated person.[152]

This affirmation manifests itself in our recognition of their humanity, their potential – this recognition understandably transcends ethnic barriers, clan superstitions or parochialism.

In a Free State is set in Uganda. The vehicle Naipaul uses to tell this tale is of course a journey, taken through Black Africa by an English homosexual who loves things African and an English 'man eater' wife of a technocrat, the new breed of expatriates to the Third World. The background to the journey is a rumoured coup and of course evil-smelling Africans, who are either performing barbaric rituals or they are power-drunk soldiers in uniform. There is the good colonel—a real colonial Englishman from the good old days who 'knows' Africans.

'You can train them so far and so far only.'[153]

Africa and Africans in a free independent state are not really of major interest to this story. What are the insights one gets into the two travelers, their psyche, their attempt to just be, without feeling threatened. They are really free-floating human beings for a change. One can only guess that Bobby comes over as humane because he has had to cope with his own alienation and isolation as a homosexual, which makes him more able to identify with 'untouchable castes', but he is an Englishman in Africa and can enjoy the best of both worlds, he can be just as dangerous in his patronising attitude to Africans as the colonel is in his contempt of them.

But to be true to the concept of 'free' in *In a Free State* it might be necessary to remember that the metaphor is scientific. Mr Walsh makes the point:

> 'A molecule in a free state presumably is freed from gravitational electrostatic and magnetic forces in the same way as Naipaul sees the traveller floating away from habit and the usual scene.'[154]

It is certainly liberating to renounce habits which are detrimental whether physically or emotionally, but the freedom which comes from simply being away from one's usual context is quite negligible if the freedom were simply license and no lasting or fundamental change resulted. There's no development, nothing has been achieved except a sense of pointless exposure and shame and probably feelings of guilt which may only compound one's alienation.

We are back to the vexed question of what indeed is a journey to accomplish? I started by suggesting that Naipaul is clarifying in his writing his life, his predicaments, and one of these was his distaste for his native land. It is ironic that Naipaul journeyed to India and gives his readers his insights in *An Area of Darkness* where he is totally revolted by the filth and because he did not find the 'balanced rural landscape of Indian Trinidad.'

'Their choice in almost everything seemed more restricted than mine; yet they were clearly the inhabitants of a big country, they had an easy unromantic comprehension of size. The landscape was hard and wrong. I could not relate it to myself. I was looking for the balanced rural landscape of Indian Trinidad.'[155]

A journey, like writing, for Naipaul, helps to clarify initial distortions and is a process of life. To William Walsh the last words:

'The fabled past, the myth, the rich and sacred sources of family certainties are finally devastatingly uncovered. The intensity of Naipaul's despair is related to the fact that in savaging India he is also savaging himself.'[156]

Whereas Harris' visionary commitment is to the cause of genuine freedom of Caribbean Man, Naipaul's conflicts make him the creator of un-free men. Naipaul's concern with ethnicity *vis à vis* African/Indian relationships is something one feels as an impediment to the genuine freedom of man.

I am suggesting that Naipaul's creative response to his schizophrenia is a form of unearthing of 'monsters,' a form of confrontation with the irrationalities which inform his art. Naipaul is using his schizophrenia to unburden his secrets, to free himself, and hopefully to free those who read him. It is cathartic, it is therapeutic, it might not be pleasant, but I suspect it is necessary for the psyche of West Indian Man to face up to these realities in his bid for wholeness.

So Naipaul perhaps in spite of himself makes creative use of his schizophrenia, for, like Virginia Woolf, he finds order in the mere act of writing about his chaos.[157]

Five

Derek Walcott: The Mulatto of Style

'...as if one general apology on
behalf of the past would supplant
imagination, would spare them
the necessity of great art.'

Derek Walcott, *Dream on Monkey Mountain*,

'What the Twilight Says: An Overture'

Derek Walcott is not only a mulatto, an ideal 'case study,' but he also epitomizes in his work the very split, which makes him 'the mulatto of style.' He is equally at home writing dialect poetry as he is in writing Standard English. Some of us would even say that he is one of the best poets writing in English at present. He is as competent in poetry as in drama, the split can even be seen in the fact that he is one of a set of twins.

There is something very affirmative about Walcott though. He exposes his life, his conflicts, his black angst, (a mirror image really of the agony of the society), but finally he purges himself through his creativity of all 'monsters' and becomes an integrated person in the process an authentic Caribbean man. This could not have been had he not the courage to confront the 'monsters' which lie under the Caribbean Man's ground of experience.

Despite temptation, he never abandons talent to despair and his collection of poetry in *Another Life* attests to this. I propose to examine *Another Life* to trace Walcott's creativity.

Another Life opens with the 'Divided Child'. We are not left long to wonder what is meant by the term, those of us of course who may not have been familiar with 'A Far Cry from Africa,'

> 'I who am poisoned with the blood of both,
> Where shall I turn, divided to the vein?
> I who have cursed
> The drunken officer of British rule, how choose
> Between this Africa and the English tongue I love?
> Betray them both or give back what they give?
> How can I turn from Africa and live.'[158]

Can take two choices of divisions from *Another Life*.

> 'The Dream of reason had produced its monster
> A prodigy of the wrong age and colour'[159]

And

> 'Mirror where a generation yearned
> For whiteness, for candour unreturned.'[160]

Whichever one chooses to examine, the question of whiteness is symbolic of the colonial's predicament in the fact of the

Imperial Powers' total domination. Militarily yes, but culturally all embracing and all inclusive. Walcott would have to wrestle in an intimate way with this dilemma since the 'prodigy' would need for his tools the language of the coloniser.

Fanon clarifies in his incisive way Walcott's dilemma:

> 'The oppressor, through the inclusive and frightening character of his authority, manages to impose on the native new ways of seeing and, in particular, a pejorative judgement with respect to his original forms of existing. This event, which is commonly designated as alienation, is naturally very important. It is found in the official texts under the name of assimilation.'[161]

So the divided child lives in two worlds, the world of the colonisers' culture—the white world, but he also lives in his black skin in a predominantly black society whose racial memories are African, whose landscape is tropical, where the sea is an ever present reality. Yet so deep is the rejection of this particular reality that:

> 'From childhood he'd considered palms
> Ignobler that imagined elms,
> The breadfruit's splayed
> Leaf coarser than the oak's
> He had prayed
> Nightly for his flesh to change,
> His dun flesh peeled white by her lightning strokes.'[162]

And no wonder, it was inevitable that a colonial should have a colonial education and if he were at all able to enter a secondary institution of learning that his teachers would be more often than not colonial representatives,

> 'I saw history through the sea-washed eyes
> Of our choleric, ginger-haired headmaster,
> Beak like an inflamed hawk's
> A lonely Englishman who loved parades,
> Sailing and Conrad's prose.'[163]

The child was always living through other men's lives, experiences and voices,

> 'A generation of slaves' children sang
> Where balmy breezes blow
> Soft winds are playing....
> Santaaa lucheeea
> Santaaa Lucheeeaa
> Steered now by Irish hands to their new epoch.
> Other men's voices
> Other men's lives and lines.'[164]

But even a divided child shares common experiences with his fellowmen. He is influenced by his parents, his friendships, his first love, his ideas of Art. He can create a mythology out of the derelict human beings who are part of his community,

> 'These dead, these derelicts,
> That alphabet of the emaciated
> They were the stars of my mythology.'[165]

There were intimations that alongside 'pragmatic methodism' and the established religions that something atavistic and gripping existed.

'One step behind the city was the bush,
One step behind the church door stood the devil.'[166]

This is one form of the tension that would produce the poet.
The two sides of the Divided Child would be reflected in the
two faces of the community,

'Traumatic, tribal
An atavism stronger than their Mass,
Stronger than chapel, whose
Tubers gripped the rooted middle-class,
Beginning where Africa began:
In the body's memory.'[167]

There is a growing recognition that this rational prodigy,
Europeanised through education, must come to terms with
the natural African part of him. There is the yearning to be
part of that life – the shallowness of racial despair then can
become the yeast, the leaven of creativity.

'The church upheld the Word, but this new Word
Was here, attainable,
To my own hand,
In the deep country it found the natural man,
Generous, rooted.
And I now yearned to suffer for that life,
I looked for some ancestral, tribal country,
I heard its clear tongue over the clean stones
Of the river, I looked from the bus window
And multiplied the bush with savages,
Speckled the leaves with jaguar and deer,
I changed those crusted boulders,
To grey, stone-lidded crocodiles,
My head shrieked with metallic, raucous parrots.

I held my breath as savages grinned,
Stalking, through the bush.'[168]

What an imaginative leap this is for the child who wanted his 'dun flesh' peeled white! It has all the impact of the celebrated Pauline conversation. Such an imaginative leap heralds the freedom to create born of the barrenness of racial despair discarded, so that

'...Like Saul, unhorsed...
That he fell in love with art,
And life began.'[169]

In 'Homage to Gregorias' Walcott celebrates not only a great friendship, but a commitment by fellow artists to pursue his peculiar art, in his own peculiar way buoyed up by a love for the island home, because of this commitment, much is said about art, but in the final analysis the medium, (Walcott's verse) is the message.

'For no one had yet written of this landscape,
That it was possible, though there were sounds
Given to its varieties of wood,
The bois-canot responded to its echo,
When the axe spoke, weeds ran up to the knee
Like bastard children, hiding in their names;
Whole generations died unchristened,
Growths hidden in green darkness, forests
Of history thickening with amnesia
So that a man's branches, naked trunk
Its roots crusted with dirt,
Swayed where it stopped, remembering another
name.'[170]

The sense of devotion to a cause, the urgency of work to be done, the doubts and questions raised about style, about originality are these.

> '...Besides the road,
> a beautiful, brown
> Indian girl in rags, Sheaves
> of brown rice held in brown,
> brittle hands, watching us
> with that earth deep darkness
> in her gaze. She was
> the new Persephone,
> dazed, ignorant,
> waiting to be named.'[171]

Two concerns of the poet are expressed, one in style and the other which has occupied Walcott in a very fundamental way, is the question of language – should the language of Caribbean writers (borrowed as it is from their former colonial masters) share in the 'the torture of articulation,' or should it be standard British English. Walcott opted for a language which had 'the force of revelation as it invented names for things; one which finally settled on the mode of inflection and which began to create an oral culture.'[172]

> 'But we were orphans of the nineteenth century,
> Sedulous to the morals of a style,
> We lived by another light,
> Victoria's orphans, bats in the banyan boughs.'[173]

This is indicative of some blindness to the needs of their community at that point in time and place. A suggestion is made here to look homeward.

'I had entered the house of literature as a houseboy.
Filched as the slum child stole,
As the young slave appropriated
Those heirlooms temptingly left
With the Victorian homilies of Noli tangere.'[174]

No more this slavish addiction to acquiring and accepting a language that even now is changing as it must. Here, too, is the call to create a language suitable to the needs of the artist. But everything has to begin with the poet's desire to write verse 'ordinary/as a tumbler of island water'. But how extraordinary is Walcott's depiction of the 'cement phoenix' the rise of Castries after the fire.

The poet paints in words, the return to some form of normality, a city which was destroyed by fire thus:

'Meanwhile to one metre, in the burnt town
Things found the memory of their former place,
That vase of roses slowly sought its centre
Like a film reeled backward, like a poltergeist reversed.
Oleographs of Christ the Sacred Heart
Sailed towards their new hooks and anchored there,
Doilies like feathers floating settled softly,
Frames drew their portraits like a closing rose,
Laces resumed their spinsterish precision
And parlours were once more varnished, sacrosanct.
Apartment blocks whitened the air,
Cul-de-sacs changed their dialect patronyms,
To boulevards and avenue,
The cement phoenix rose.'[175]

This is indeed extraordinary verse, it is as though the poet waves the magic wand of his words to rebuild a city indeed—

this is verse 'as crisp as sand.' There is the sense of movement, things, gracefully falling into place, words like 'slowly sought', 'film reeled,' 'sailed,' 'feathers floating,' 'settled softly.' The touch is light and elegant. The poet is seeking his style and delineating his method at one and the same time, the process is continuous.

Walcott is impatient with the idea of history as time past, he has something in common with Wilson Harris who thinks,

'Within each prisoner of history is an attachment involuntary perhaps, but concrete to the very premises of his age. How could it be otherwise, when those premises are all he possesses or is possessed by.'[176]

So Walcott conjures up a Caribbean hell to send the historians to:

'Miasma, acedia, the enervations of damp,
As the teeth of the mould gnaw, greening the
Carious stump,
Of the beaten, corrugated silver of the marsh light,
Where the red heron hides, without a secret,
As the cordage of mangrove tightens,
Bland water to bland sky,
Heavy and sodden as canvas,
Where the pirogue foundered with its caved in stomach,
(a hulk, trying hard to look like
a paleolithic, half gnawed memory of pre-history)
as the too green acid grasses set the salt teeth on edge,
acids and russets and water-coloured water,
let the historian go mad there from thirst.'[177]

Having consigned the historian to this Caribbean Hell, Walcott observes: 'the tired slave vomits his past.' Is he possessed by it or does he possess it? For Walcott, one must become a child again, the child can hear what the historian cannot, because what is demanded is an ability to enter imaginatively into what Harris calls 'the real reverses the human spirit has endured.'

'A new hunger – a new subsistence of memory –
Comes into play wherein both sovereign statecraft
And primitive king are implicated in the dust of
History, blowing as it were towards a new terrifying,
yet liberating 'immaterial' conception.
An art of fiction where the agents of time begin to subsist
upon the real reverses the human spirit has endured
the real chasm of pain it has entered, rather than the
apparent consolidation, victories and battles it has
won.'[178]

So when Walcott invests in a child the ability to hear everything 'that the historian cannot hear' it begins to make sense.

'That child who sets his half shell afloat
In the brown creek that is Rampanalgas River
My son first, then two daughters –
Towards the roar of waters,
Towards the Atlantic with a dead almond leaf for a soul
With a twig for a mast,
Was, like his father, this child,
A child without history, without knowledge of its pre-world
Only the knowledge of water runnelling rocks
And the desperate whelk that grips the rock's outcrop
Like a man whom the waves can never wash overboard;
That child who puts the shell's bowl to his ear,
Hears nothing, hears everything

That the historian cannot hear, the howls
Of grandfathers drowned
In that intricately swivelled Babel,
Hears the fellaheen, the Madrasi, the Mandigo, the
Ashanti,
Yes, and hears also the echoing green fissures of
Canton,
And thousand without longing for this other shore,
By the mid tablets of the Indian Provinces,
Robed ghostly white and brown, the twigs of uplifted
hands,
Of manacles, mantras, of a thousand kaddishes,
Whorled, drilling into the shell
See, in the evening light of the saffron, sacred
Benares,
How they are lifting like herons,
Robed ghostly white and brown,
And the crossing of water has erased their memories.
And the sea, which is always the same,
Accepts them,
And the shore, which is always the same,
Accepts them.
In the shallop of the shell,
In the round prayer,
In the palate of the conch
In the dead sail of the almond leaf
Are all of the voyages.'[179]

But Walcott has a word for those who glamorize cruelty, who
make of conquest, something glorious, who believe that at
least there, something happened—perhaps they will absolve
us if we begin again if we use the concept of the tabula rasa
– a clean slate – let's see if we cannot improve on those
lessons of history:

'They will absolve us, perhaps, if we begin again,
From what we have always known, nothing
From the carnal slime of the garden
From the incarnate subtlety of the snake,
From the Egyptian moment of the heron's foot
On the mud's entablature,
By this augury of ibises
Flying at evening from the melting trees,
While the silver hammered charger of the marsh light
Brings towards us, again and again, in beaten scrolls,
Nothing, then nothing
And then nothing.'[180]

So that is the challenge, we have the ability (or rather we must)
there is no choice.

'Man's nature his passions, and anxieties are a
Cultural product, as a matter of fact man himself
Is the most important creation and achievement of
The continuous human effort, the record of which
We call history.'[181]

Reading Walcott's works one cannot but be impressed by
the fact that his concept of love is the very Christian one of
caring, caring for one's fellow man in the profoundest way.
This element of caring takes the form of meticulous care in
his art, and regard for his Muse.

These are very moving lines, reminiscent of Wordsworth's
autobiographical lines in the Prelude.

About the August of my fourteenth year
I lost myself somewhere above a valley
Owned by a spinster farmer, my dead father's friend.

At the hill's edge there was a scarp
With bushes and boulders stuck in its side.
Afternoon light ripened the valley.
Rifling smoke climbed from small labourers' houses
And I dissolved into a trance.
I was seized by a pity more profound
Than my young body could bear, I climbed
With the labouring smoke,
I drowned in labouring breakers of bright cloud,
Then uncontrollably I began to weep,
Inwardly, without tears, with a serene extinction
Of all sense; I felt compelled to kneel,
I wept for nothing and for everything,
I wept for the earth for the hill under my knees
For the grass, the pebbles, for the cooking smoke
Above the labourers' houses like a cry,
For the unheard avalanches of white cloud,
But 'darker grows the valley, more and more forgetting.'
For their light still shine through the hovels like litmus,
The smoking lamp still slowly says its prayer,
The poor still move behind their tinted scrim,
The taste of water is still shared everywhere,
But in that ship of night, locked in together,
Through which, like chains, a little light might leak,
Something still fastens us forever to the poor.'[182]

Walcott is not only meticulous about his art, but always he is
conscious of his creative call as a Caribbean artist.

'The smell of our own speech,
The smell of baking bread,
Of drizzled asphalt, this
Odorous cedar. After the rain
The rinsed shingles shone,
Resinous as the smell of country sweat,

Of salt crusted fishermen.'[183]

He is faithful to the scents, scenes and images of the Caribbean. Which islander cannot but recognise in these lines nostalgic memories of the countryside after a tropical shower?

But Walcott can also write of young love with all the naivety, and freshness of a true romantic, "Mother, I am in love," a revelation, a sense of heightened awareness, all the fear and trembling and wonder of love is captured in some of these lines.

> '...I could be happy,
> just because today is Sunday. No, for more.
> Then Sundays, smiling, carried in both hands
> a towelled dish bubbling with the good life
> whose fervour steaming, beaded her clear brow,
> from which damp skeins were brushed,
> and ladled out her fullness to the brim.'[184]

The imaginative impulse is more demanding than the simple demands of the lover.

> 'And which of them in time would be betrayed,
> Was never questioned by that poetry
> Which breathed within the evening naturally,
> But by the noble treachery of art
> That looks for fear when it is least afraid,
> That coldly takes the pulse beat of the heart,
> In happiness; that praised its need to die
> To the bring candour of the evening sky,
> That preferred love to immortality;
> So every step increased that subtlety
> Which hoped that their two bodies could be made

One body of immortal metaphor
The hand she held already had betrayed
Them by its longing for describing her.
So one grows older and wiser.
A man lives half of life,
The second half is memory.'[185]

The mature Walcott recognises that young love, evanescent and
inspiring, lays the foundation on which mature relationships
develop:

'And do I still love her, as I love you?
I have loved all women who have evolved from her,
Fired by two marriages
To have her gold ring true.'[186]

The maturing Walcott, recognises and accepts the essential
role of woman in the process of moving to psychic health.
It is the recognition that the ability to love is an essential
ingredient of creativity.

Inevitably for the divided children of the British Empire, the
rejection of his 'original forms of existing' would imply an
acceptance of the colonisers' form of existing. But this is
on the psychological plane; there have been more basic and
fundamental reasons for the Caribbean writers' need for exile.
The hard economic facts remain true even today. The artist
cannot make a living in the Caribbean, his books are not
published here. The attitude of newly independent countries
to serious art is unimaginative to say the least, thus there were
and still are practical reasons in favour of exile.

But the agony of departure is no less real.

'Earth-heart, I prayed,
Nerves of raw fibre,
Uproot me, yet
Let what I have sworn to love not feel betrayed
When I must go, and, if I must go,
Make of my heart an ark
Let my ribs bear
All, doubled by
Memory, down to the emerald fly
Marrying this hand, and be
The image of a young man on a pier
His heart a ship within a ship within
a ship, a bottle where his wharf, these
rotting roofs, this sea, sail, sealed in glass.'[187]

The poet is understandably concerned that removal from the sustaining source of his inspiration would result in the drying up of his creativity. He needs his native country, his natural surroundings.

'A native country is a sort of second body,
Another enveloping organism to give the will
Definition.'[188]

The poet expresses gratitude that he was touched by poverty; uncertainly, by other's sadness, such is the meat of the poet, the motivation the preparation for taking off on the adventure which is the life—art.

'...you faced the blank page,
and trembled, you had learnt by heart
the monotonous scrawl of the beaches
for years trying to reach you,
delivering the same message, Go,

in the crab's carapace from which the crabshell
had vanished, in eyes ground the colour of the sea-stone.
Their lives slipped into your own
Like letters under a door.'[189]

The artist also needs to be protected from himself—from his
own sensitivity and pain—he needs like the crab, a protective
covering this 'crab's carapace' might be a metaphor for the
artist in exile, at least his anonymity is part of the pleasure of
exile—his distancing, physically and spiritually from both the
anguish and the attraction of his native land. His separation
is his protection, at least for a time.

'The islands were a string of barges towed
nowhere,
Every view
Assembling itself to say farewell.'[190]

And *Another Life* begins:

'And I left there that morning with a last look
At things that would not say what they once meant.'[191]

But not for Walcott the long exile from home.

Walcott's *Another Life* is a journey through time and space,
but inner space has been the more relevant experience for
the reader, for we lived within the poet's skin, we shared his
life, his longings, his triumphs, and his failures and we also
share in the resolution to his challenges. For indeed he has
overcome, indeed he is home at last.

And how does this particular pilgrim come to his rest!!

'Gregorias liste, lit, we were the light of the world!'

An unmistakable note of triumph, balancing one's gains and losses and coming out of it all with more to one's credit than one was led to expect. There is a sense in which Walcott has experienced like the molecule in a 'free state a floating away from the habitual gravitational pull' but he has nothing to be ashamed of

> '...A sun that stands back from
> the fire of itself, not shamed, prizing
> its shadow, watching it blaze!'[192]

But to arrive at this realisation after all the anguish and the bitterness, the poet had to purge himself of his anger and his hate,

> 'I have swallowed all my hates'[193]

He says, he has experienced the cleansing purifying tears which lead to renewal and regeneration:

> 'And on that hill, that evening,
> When the deep valley grew blue with forgetting,
> Why did I weep,
> Why did I kneel,
> Whom did I thank?
> I knelt because I was my mother,
> I was the well of the world,
> I wore the stars on my skin,
> I endured no reflections,
> My sign was water,
> Tears and the sea

My sign was Janus,
I saw with twin heads,
And everything I say is contradicted.'[194]

In what sense is the poet 'home'? In Walcott's poem 'Homecoming' the poet faces up to the realisation that the reality of his physical return to his native land was at variance with his spiritual return. There he was in fact at home but not at home, neither at ease, not in harmony with himself. So what has happened in 'Another Life' to suggest that some form of equilibrium has been achieved?

Being at home presupposes that one loves, one is authentic and this authenticity is a constructive process, a process which involves an honest and unashamed acceptance of the turgid waters of the unconscious, it indeed takes courage to confess to one's self hate and rejection. To make of these negations something creative, it is the clarity with which Walcott could pinpoint his peculiar schizophrenia and see it as his mission to make creative use of it. The pursuit of his goal has helped his audience particularly his Caribbean audience, to move with him to the recognition that Caribbean man's schizophrenia is part and parcel of man's cultural schizophrenia.

This is what Harris has to say about one's 'native land':

> 'One's native land (and the other's) is always crumbling
> With a capacity of vision which rediscovers the process
> To be not foul and destructive, but actually the constructive
> Secret of all creation, wherever one happens to be.'[195]

Thus Walcott has come home because he has the vision, the

imagination to make nothing, something.

'If there was nothing, there was everything to be made.
With this prodigious ambition one began.'[196]

To his everlasting credit it could be said that the seeds of this
ambition were also watered with love and it is this love which
has made his 'homecoming' possible.

Here is what another pilgrim in another country has to say
about this state of being 'at home':

'The way home we seek is that condition of man's being
at home in the world which is called love and which we
term democracy.'[197]

Ralph Ellison knows of what he speaks. Walcott comes 'home'
in *Another Life*. Walcott is now:

'...this neither proud nor ashamed bastard,
this hybrid West Indian.'[198]

Personal integration has been attained.

Conclusion

'Yet when we look at the human we must be prepared not to overlook these obsessions but to work them into the structure of art so that all these levels of man are present. It is the only way we can come close to the real power of man by showing the interaction of all the levels of his life, thereby not only baring his conflict, but the rhythms within the welter of his existence.'

Wilson Harris[199]

The quest of the Caribbean writer has revealed among other things that in making creative use of his schizophrenia he has been coming to grips with what essentially is man's cultural schizophrenia. For although exile/homecoming would have special meaning and significance for Caribbean people in a Caribbean context, man's being at home in his world is a question of universal significance in our time.

Man's sense of being at home in the world of his making is fundamental to our existence. So much that is negative and psychologically destructive to human life is a result of the alienation of modern man. Homecoming is indeed a state of consciousness, an arrival at some point of awareness, an equilibrium, a harmonious state whence all or most conflicts have been satisfactorily resolved.

Brathwaite, Naipaul, Harris and Walcott are the Magellans and

Columbuses of the Caribbean psyche. They have made the discovery that we as Caribbean people have been the victims of 'constitutional handicaps' in facing our stress situations, the symptoms of our schizophrenia have been inauthenticity, mimicry and alienation. The constitutional handicaps with which we have been meeting our stress are among others, racial despair, the sense of being in a wrong place, our distorted sense of history, failure sometimes to recognise our African past. These writers have caused us to see ourselves anew. We have been made to feel more at ease with ourselves, by being forced to confront our 'conflicts and obsessions'. Caribbean writing, after these writers, must necessarily be different. They have by their courage, dedication and sincerity done what no other segment of society has done or could do with the thoroughness and insight which they alone could.

They have had the honesty and vision to bring to the light of day these hidden subterranean forces which precipitate the disintegration of emotional stability, so characteristic of the schizophrenic. Lest we believe that this is all they have unearthed, let me hasten to add that by their works we shall know them: that the strength of the writers and their society have been the fact that out of chaos they have proceeded to create something that is essentially a tribute to the Caribbean people and their experience—a literature that is undoubtedly Caribbean, and whole.

Endnotes

Abstract of Thesis

1. Derek Walcott, *What the Twilight Says: An Overture*. "Dream On Monkey Mountain and Other Plays". (Johnathan Cape, 1972). p. 12.

Introduction

2. The title of a Caribbean History series edited by Edward Brathwaite, Patricia Patterson and James Carnegie. (Longman Caribbean, 1968).

3. Quoted from George Lamming's address to graduates of the University of the West Indies, Cave Hill, 1980-02-06.

4. Wilson Harris. *Tradition, the Writer and Society*. (New Beacon Publication, 1967). p.3.

5. Ibid, p. 31.

6. Ibid, p. 31.

7. Ibid, p. 31.

8. Michael Gilkes. *Wilson Harris and the Caribbean Novel*. (Longman Caribbean 1975). p. 7.

9. Frantz Fanon. *Toward the African Revolution*. (Penguin Books, 1975). p. 48.

10. Frantz Fanon quoted in Gilkes's *Wilson Harris and the Caribbean Novel*. Introduction, p. xi.

11. Martin Carter quoted in Gilkes's *Wilson Harris and the Caribbean Novel*. Introduction, p. xi.

12. Michael Gilkes, *Wilson Harris and the Caribbean Novel*. Introduction,

p. xi.

13. Derek Walcott. "What the Twilight Says: An Overture". Preface to *Dream on Monkey Mountain and Other Plays*. (Jonathan Cape, 1972). p. 10.

14. Ibid, p. 12.

15. Seepersad Naipaul. *The Adventures of Gurudeva and other Stories*. (Andre Deutsch, 1971) Foreword by his son V.S. Naipaul, p. 22.

16. Wilson Harris. *Reflection and Vision*. Lecture. (Dangaroo Press 1975). p. 18.

17. George Lamming. Address to Graduates, University of the West Indies, Cave Hill, 1980-02-06. op. cit.

18. David Stafford-Clark. *Psychiatry Today*. (Penguin, 1952). p. 102.

19. Derek Walcott. "What the Twilight Says: An Overture". Preface to *Dream on Monkey Mountain and Other Plays*. op cit., p. 4.

20. R. D. Laing. *The Politics of Experience and the Bird of Paradise*. (Penguin Books, 1967). p. 86.

21. Ibid, p. 95.

22. Ibid, p. 107.

23. R. D. Laing. *The Divided Self: A Study of Samity and Madness*. (Tavistock Publications, 1960). p. 15.

24. Derek Walcott. "What the Twilight Says: An Overture". op. cit. p. 7.

25. Garth St. Omer. *J. Blackbarn and the Masqueraders*. (Faber and Faber, 1972), p. 93.

26. Ibid, p. 93.

27. V.S. Naipaul,.Introduction to *The Adventures of Gurudeva and Other Stories*. op. cit. Foreword. p. 18.

28. Derek Walcott. *Homecoming: Anse La Raye, the Gulf*. (Jonathan Cape, 1969). p. 50.

29. Wilson Harris. *The Eye of the Scarecrow*. (Faber and Faber, 1965). p. 10.

30. Derek Walcott. *Homecoming: Anse La Raye, The Gulf*. (Jonathan Cape, 1969). p. 50.

31. Derek Walcott. "What the Twilight Says: An Overture". op. cit. p.

17.

32. Ibid, p. 19.

33. Wilson Harris. Reflection and Vision. Lecture. (Dangaroo Press, 1975). op. cit., p. 15.

One
Creative Use of Schizophrenia: The Interior Life of Poetry; The Outward Life of Action and Dialect

34. Derek Walcott. "What the Twilight Says: An Overture". *Dream on Monkey Mountain and Other Plays*. (Jonathan Cape, 1972). p. 12.

35. C.L.R. James. *The Artist in the Caribbean*. (C.L.R. James Radical America, Vol. 14, No. 4, May 1970). p. 61

36. Heidegger. Quoted by C.L.R. James. Appendix, Introduction to Tradition and the West Indian Novel. *Tradition, the Writer and Society*. (New Beacon Books, 1967). p. 70.

37. Derek Walcott. *Another Life*. (London Cape, 1973), p. 77.

38. Gerald Moore. *The Chosen Tongue*. (Longmans Green & Co. Ltd., 1959). Introduction, xviii.

39. Edward Brathwaite. *Islands* .(OUP, 1969). p. 64.

40. Ibid, p. 66-7.

41. Derek Walcott. "What the Twilight Says: An Overture". op. cit., p. 17.

42. Derek Walcott. *Joker of Seville*. (Jonathan Cape, 1972).

43. Michael Fabre. The poetical journey of Derek Walcott. *Commonwealth Literature and the Modern World*. (Aarhus, 1971). p. 66.

44. Derek Walcott. *Another Life*. op. cit., p. 152.

45. Ibid, p. 74.

46. Wilson Harris Interview Contact Newspaper, March 1980, p. 18.

47. Ibid, p. 18.

48. Wilson Harris. *Tradition, the Writer and Society*. op. cit., p. 14.

49. Ibid, p. 14.

50. Wilson Harris. *The Eye of the Scarecrow*. (Faber and Faber, 1965). p. 97.

51. Ibid, p. 97.

Two

Brathwaite and the African Presence in the Caribbean

52. E.L. Brathwaite. "Roots". *Bim* Vol X, No. 37. (July-December 1963). p. 10.

53. Victor Turner. *The Forest of Symbols: Aspects of Ndembu Ritual*. (Cornell University Press, 1967). p. 94.

54. E.L. Brathwaite. "The Arrivants", *Rights of Passage*. (OUP, 1973). p. 10.

55. Victor Turner. *The Forest of Symbols*. p. 98.

56. E.L. Brathwaite. *Rights of Passage*. (OUP, 1967), p. 13.

57. Ibid, p. 15.

58. Ibid, p. 34

59. Ibid, p. 37.

60. Ibid, p. 38.

61. Ibid, p. 41.

62. Ibid, p. 76.

63. Gordon Rohlehr. "Blues and Rebellion": Edward Brathwaite's Rights of Passage. *Critics on Caribbean Literature*. (Geoge Allen and Unwin, 1978), p. 63.

64. E.L.Brathwaite. *Masks*. (OUP, 1968). p. 3.

65. Ibid, p. 16

66. Ibid, p. 40

67. Ibid, p. 66

68. Ibid, p. 74

69. Orlando Patterson. *The Children of Sisyphus*. (London, New Authors, 1954).

70. James Baldwin. *Tell Me How Long the Train's Been Gone*. (London,

Joseph 1968). Brathwaite uses the quotations as a foreword in *Islands*.

71. E.L. Brathwaite. *Islands*. (OUP, 1969) p. 4-5.

72. Ibid, "Jou'vert". p. 113.

73. Ibid, "Caliban". p. 37-88.

74. Ibid, "Rites" p. 43-44.

75. Ibid, "Ancestors". p. 82.

76. E.L. Brathwaite. "Jou'vert". *Islands*. op. cit., p. 113.

77. George Lamming, Novel by George Lamming.

78. Martin Carter. Such early work of Martin Carter including the famous *Poems of Resistance* (1954) are collected in *Poems of Succession* (London:New Beacon Books, 1977).

Three

Wilson Harris and Character Fulfilment

79. Wilson Harris. *Tradition, the Writer and Society*. (New Beacon Books, 1967). p. 29.

80. Ibid.

81. Ibid.

82. Ibid.

83. Carl Jung. The Collected Works. *Alchemical Studies*. (Routledge and Kegan Paul, 1960). p. 321.

84. Wilson Harris. *Reflections and Vision*, Lecture. (Dangaroo Press, 1975). p. 18.

85. Ibid.

86. C.L.R. James. *C.L.R. James' Radical America*. Mariners, Renegades and Castaways. (1953). p. 92.

87. Wilson Harris. *Reflections and Vision*. op. cit., p. 9.

88. Ibid.

89. C.L.R. James. *C.L.R. James' Radical America*. Philosopy and Modem Society. Excerpt from Modern Politics (1960), p. 10.

90. Wilson Harris. *Tradition, the Writer and Society.* (New Beacon Books, 1967), p. 60.

91. C.L.R. James. *C.L.R. James' Radical America.* Philosopy and Modern Society. p. 10.

92. Wilson Harris. Author's Note. *The Whole Armour and The Secret Ladder* .(Faber and Faber, 1973). p. 8.

93. C.LR. James. *C.L.R. James' Radical America.* Mariners, Renegades and Castaways (1970). p. 81.

94. C.L.R. James. The Artist in the Caribbean. *C.L.R. James' Radical America.* (1970). p. 63.

95. Peterson/Rutherford. *Enigma of Values.* (Aarhus, 1975). p. 15.

96. Wilson Harris. Interior of the Novel. *National Identity.* (Heineman 1970). p. 140.

97. W. B. Gallie. *Philosophy and the Historical Understanding.* (Chatto and Windus, 1964). p. 103.

98. Wilson Harris. *The Eye of the Scarecrow.* (Faber and Faber, 1965). p. 10.

99. Wilson Harris. *Eternity to Season.* (Guyana, 1954). p. 11.

100. Jacques Monod. *Chance and Necessity.* (Collins, 1972) pp. 166-167.

101. Petersen/Rutherford. *Enigma of Values.* (Aarhus, 1975). p .9.

102. L. De Broglie. *Physics and Metaphysics.* (Harper N.Y. 1960). p. 264.

103. Wilson Harris. *The Whole Armour.* (Faber and Faber, 1962). p. 43.

104. Kenneth Ramchand. *An Introduction to the Study of West Indian Literature.* (Thomas Nelson and Sons Ltd., 1976). p. 164.

105. Wilson Harris. *The Secret Ladder.* (Faber and Faber, 1962). p. 169.

106. Wilson Harris. *The Whole Armour.* (Faber and Faber, 1962). p. 44.

107. Wilson Harris. *Palace of the Peacock.* (Faber and Faber, 1960). p. 40.

108. Wilson Harris. *Tumatumari.* (Faber and Faber. 1968). p. 102.

109. Wilson Harris. *Da Silva da Silva's Cultivated Wilderness.* (Fabe and Faber, 1977). p. 6.

110. Wilson Harris. *Tumatumari.* (Faber and Faber, 1968). p. 152.

111. Wilson Harris. *Genesis of the Clowns.* (Faber and Faber, 1977). p. 99.

112. Wilson Harris. *Tumatumari*. (Faber and Faber, 1968). p. 152.

113. Wilson Harris. *The Secret Ladder*. (Faber and Faber, 1963). p. 39.

114. Ibid, p. 51.

115. Ibid, p. 68.

116. Ibid, p. 61.

117. Michael Gilkes. *Wilson Harris and the Caribbean Novel*. (Longman Caribbean, 1975). p. 103.

118. Wilson Harris. *Genesis of the Clowns*. (Faber and Faber, 1977). p. 94.

119. Carl G. Jung. The Collected Works. *Alchemical Studies*. op. cit., p. 219.

120. Ibid, p. 333.

121. Wilson Harris. *The Whole Armour*, (Faber and Faber, 1962). p. 15.

122. Wilson Harris. *Palace of the Peacock*. (Faber and Faber, 1960). p. 17.

123. C.L.R. James. *C.L.R. James' Radical America*, Mariners, Renegades and Castaways. (1953). p. 82.

124. Wilson Harris. *Palace of the Peacock*. (Faber and Faber, 1960). p. 56.

125. Ibid, p. 140.

126. Ibid, p. 151.

Four

Naipaul's Dilemma

127. Derek Walcott. "What the Twilight Says: An Overture". *Dream on Monkey Mountain and Other Plays*. (Jonathan Cape, 1972). p. 12.

128. Ibid, p. 18.

129. V.S. Naipaul. "The Tramp at Piraeus". *In a Free State*. (Andre Deutsch, 1971). p. 11.

130. William Walsh. *V.S. Naipaul*. (Oliver and Boyd, 1973). p. 25.

131. Erich Fromm. *Fear of Freedom*. (Routledge and Kegan Paul Ltd., 1960). p. 225.

132. Ibid, p. 225.

133. V.S. Naipaul. "The Tramp at Piraeus". *In a Free State*. (Andre Deutsch, 1971), pp. 11-12.

134. Ibid, pp. 11-12.

135. V.S. Naipaul. "One Out of Many". *In a Free State*. (Andre Deutsch, 1971). p. 6.

136. Ibid, p. 25.

137. Ibid, p. 58.

138. Ibid, p. 58.

139. Ibid, p. 40.

140. Ibid, p. 40.

141. Ibid, p. 42.

142. Ibid, p. 39.

143. Ibid, p. 39.

144. Ibid, p. 61.

145. William Walsh. *V.S. Naipaul*. (Oliver Boyd, 1973). p. 59.

146. Ibid, p. 333.

147. A.C. Derrick. *Naipaul's Technique as a Novelist*. (Journal of Commonwealth Literature, No.7, July 1969). pp. 32-3.

148. Gordon Rohler. "The Ironic Approach". *The Islands in Between*. (OUP. 1968)/ op. cit., pp. 132-8.

149. V.S. Naipaul. *The Loss of El Dorado*. (Andre Deutsch, 1967). p. 25.

150. Erich Fromm. *Fear of Freedom*, (Routledge and Kegan Paul Ltd. 1960), p. 28.

151. Ibid, p. 91.

152. Ibid, p. 222.

153. V.S. Naipaul. "In a Free State". *In a Free State*. (Andre Deutsch, 1971), p. 214.

154. William Walsh. *V.S. Naipaul*. (Oliver and Boyd, 1973). p. 69.

155. V.S. Naipaul. *An Area of Darkness*. (Andre Deutsch, 1971).

156. William Walsh, V.S. Naipaul. (Olive and Boyd, 1973).

157. Virginia Woolf. See *A Writer's Diary*.

Five
Derek Walcott: The Mulatto of Style

158. Derek Walcott. *In a Green Night.* (Jonathan Cape, 1962). p. 18.

159. Derek Walcott. *Another Life.* (Jonathan Cape, 1973). p. 3.

160. Ibid, p. 3.

161. Frantz Fanon. *Toward the African Revolution.* (Penguin, 1964). p. 48.

162. Derek Walcott. *Another Life.* (Jonathan Cape, 1973). p. 6.

163. Ibid, p. 70.

164. Ibid, pp. 105-6

165. Ibid, p. 22.

166. Ibid, p. 25.

167. Ibid, pp. 24-5.

168. Ibid, p. 42.

169. Ibid, p. 44.

170. Ibid, pp. 53-54.

171. Ibid, pp. 76-7.

172. Derek Walcott. "What the Twilight Says: An Overture." *Dream on Monkey Mountain and Other Plays.* (Jonathan Cape, 1972). p. 17.

173. Derek Walcott. *Another Life.* (Jonathan Cape, 1973). p .77.

174. Ibid, p. 77.

175. Ibid, p. 83.

176. Wilson Harris. Benito Cereno, Enigma of Values. (Dangaroo Press 1975) p. 44.

177. Derek Walcott. *Another Life.* (Jonathan Cape, 1973). p. 141.

178. Wilson Harris. Interior of the Novel. *National Identity.* (Heinemann 1970). p. 141.

179. Derek Walcott. *Another Life.* (Jonathan Cape, 1973). pp. 143-4.

180. Ibid, pp. 144-5

181. Erich Fromm. *Fear of Freedom.* (Routledge and Kegan Paul Ltd., 1960). p. 9.

182. Derek Walcott. *Another Life.* (Jonathan Cape, 1973). pp. 42-3.

183. Ibid, p. 75.

184. Ibid, p. 92.

185. Ibid, p. 93.

186. Ibid, p. 94.

187. Ibid, p. 101.

188. Santayana. *The Life of Reason*, Volume III, Reason in Religion. (N.Y. and London, 1905) Chapter X, Piety. p. 185.

189. Derek Walcott. *Another Life*. (Jonathan Cape, 1973). pp. 109-110.

190. Ibid, p. 111.

191. Ibid, p. 111.

192. Ibid, p. 113.

193. Ibid, p. 140.

194. Ibid, p. 113.

195. Wilson Harris. *The Eye of the Scarecrow*. (Faber and Faber, 1965). p. 10.

196. Derek Walcott. "What the Twilight Says: An Overture". op. cit., p. 4.

197. Ralph Ellison. *Shadow and Act*. (New American Library, 1953). p. 114.

198. Derek Walcott. *Another Life*. (Jonathan Cape, 1973)

Conclusion

199. Wilson Harris. "Form and Realism in the West Indian Artist". *Tradition, the Writer and Society*. (New BeaconBooks, 1967). p. 14.

Bibliography

BALDWIN, James. *Tell Me How Long The Train's Been Gone*. London: Joseph, 1968.

BAUGH, Edward. *Critics on Caribbean Literature*. George Allen and Unwin Ltd., 1978.

BRATHWAITE, E.L. 'Roots' *Bim*. Vol X, No. 37 (July December 1963) The Arrivants, Oxford University Press, 1973.

BURLAND, C.A. *The Arts of the Alchemists*. Weidenfield and Nicholson, 1905.

COOMBS, Orde. *Is Massa Day Dead*. Anchor Press/Doubleday, 1974.

DE BROGLE, L. *Physics and Metaphysics*. Harper, NX 1960.

DERRICK, A.C. "Naipaul's Technique as a novelist". *Commonwealth Literature*, VII (July 1969), 32-33.

ELLISON, Ralph. *Shadow and Act*. Signet, 1966.

FABRE, Michael. "The Poetical Journey of Derek Walcott". *Commonwealth Literature and the Modern World*.(July 1971).

FANON, Frantz. *Toward the African Revolution*. Penguin Books, 1967.

FROMM, Erich. *The Fear of Freedom*. Routledge and Kegan Paul, 1960.

GALLIE, W.B. *Philosophy and the Historical Understanding*. Chatto & Windus, 1964.

GILKES, Michael. *Wilson Harris and the Caribbean Novel*, Longman Caribbean, 1975.

GOODWIN, K.L. *National Identity*. Heinemann, 1970.

HARRIS, Wilson. *History Fable and Myth in the Caribbean and Guiana*. Lectures Guyana: 1970

HARRIS, Wilson. *Tradition the Writer and Society*. New Beacon Books, 1967.

HARRIS, Wilson. *Da Silva da Silva's Cultivated Wilderness*. Faber and Faber,

1977.

HARRIS, Wilson. *The Eye of the Scarecrow.* Faber and Faber, 1965

HARRIS, Wilson. "Interior of the Novel." *National Identity.* Heinemann, 1970.

HARRIS, Wilson. *Eternity to Season.* Guyana 1965.

HARRIS, Wilson. *Tumatumari.* Faber and Faber, 1968.

HARRIS, Wilson. *The Secret Ladder.* Faber and Faber, 1962.

HARRIS, Wilson. *The Whole Armour.* Faber and Faber, 1962.

HARRIS, Wilson. *Ascent to Omai.* Faber and Faber, 1970.

HAZLITT, William. *English Comic Writer.* J.M. Dent and Sons Ltd., 1910.

HESSE, Herman. *Steppenwolf.* Penguin Books, 1965.

JAMES, C.L.R. *C.L.R. James Radical America.* Detroit Printing Co. op, 1970.

JUNG, C.G. *Collected Works.* London: Routledge and Kegan Paul, 1953.

LAING, R.D. *The Divided Self.* Tavistock Publications, 1961a

LAING, R.D. *The Points of Experience and The Bird of Paradise.* Penguin Books, 1967.

MINDLESS, H. *Laughter and Liberation.* Nash Publishers, 1971.

MONOD, Jacques. *Change and Necessity.* Collins, 1972.

MOORE, Gerald. *The Chosen Tongue.* Longman's Green and Co. Ltd., 1969.

NAIPAUL V.S. *In a Free State.* Andre Deutsch, 1971

NAIPAUL V.S. *The Loss of Eldorado.* Andre Deutsch, 1964.

NAIPAUL, V.S. *An Area of Darkness.* Andre Deutsch, 1964.

PATTERSON, Orlando. *The Children of Sisyphus.* Andre Deutsch, 1964.

RAMCHAND, Kenneth.*An Introduction to the Study of West Indian Literature, The West Indian Novel and Its Background.* Thomas Nelson and Sons Ltd., 1976.

SANTAYANA. *The Life of Reason.* Vol III NY and London: 1905.

STAFFORD CLARK, David. *Psychiatry Today.* Penguin 1961.

TURNER, Victor. *The Forests of Symbols, Aspeects of Ndembu Ritual.* N.Y: Ithaca Press, 1967.

VAN GENNEP, A. *Rites of Passage.* Routledge and Kegan Paul, 1960.

WALCOTT, Derek. *Another Life.* London: Cape, 1973

WALCOTT, Derek. *Dream on Moneky Mountain and Other Plays*. London: Jonathan Cape, 1972.

WALCOTT, Derek. *The Castaway and other Poems*. London: Cape 1962

WALCOTT, Derek. *In A Green Night*. Jonathan Cape, 1962.

WALSH, William. *V.S. Naipaul*. Oliver and Boyd, 1973.

www.ingramcontent.com/pod-product-compliance
Lightning Source LLC
Chambersburg PA
CBHW060403090426
42734CB00011B/2248